Are You Managing Purchasing?

ALLIED DUNBAR

Other Books in the Series

ARE YOU MANAGING?
A Guide to Good Management
Peter Stemp

ARE YOU MANAGING YOUR HEALTH?
A Guide to a Balanced Lifestyle
Dr H. Beric Wright

Allied Dunbar

Allied Dunbar is one of Britain's largest financial groups, offering services which include life assurance, personal pensions and unit trust investment. With more than one million clients and over £8 billion funds under management, Allied Dunbar has been recognised as one of the leading growth companies and innovators in the UK personal financial services industry.

There are over 8,000 Allied Dunbar people, comprising a large professional sales force backed by a team of managers and support staff. Allied Dunbar's business success is based on sound management practices and the commitment of all its people.

ALLIED DUNBAR

Are You Managing Purchasing?

by

Malcolm Jones

nb

NICHOLAS BREALEY
PUBLISHING
LONDON

First published by
Nicholas Brealey Publishing Limited in 1992
156 Cloudesley Road
London N1 0EA

in association with
The Industrial Society
48 Bryanston Square
London W1H 7LN
Telephone: 071 262 2401

ISBN 1 85788 002 1

© Allied Dunbar Financial Services Limited 1992

Illustrations by 'Sax'

All rights reserved. No part of this publication may be reproduced, stored in a retrieval system, or transmitted, in any form or by any means, electronic, mechanical, photocopying, recording and/or otherwise without the prior written permission of the publishers. This book may not be lent, resold, hired out or otherwise disposed of by way of trade in any form, binding or cover other than that in which it is published, without prior consent of the publishers.

British Library Cataloguing in Publication Data
A catalogue record for this book is available from the British Library.

Allied Dunbar Assurance plc
Allied Dunbar Centre
Swindon SN1 1EL
Tel: 0793 514514

Typeset by Midlands Book Typesetting Ltd.
Printed and bound in Great Britain by
Billings Book Plan Ltd., Worcester.

ABOUT THE AUTHORS

Malcolm Jones is the Group Purchasing and Distribution Services Manager for Allied Dunbar. His management responsibilities come through purchasing, graphics and warehousing. He has a background in purchasing of over twenty years and was instrumental in developing the current purchasing strategy at Allied Dunbar. He is a corporate member of the IPS and has a BTec in Management Studies.

Paul Murphy is Group Purchasing Manager. After graduating, he joined EMI as a trainee in purchasing, becoming involved in areas as diverse as defence electronics and the music industry. Paul's team is helping Allied Dunbar enhance its reputation in the purchasing profession, with the aim of increasing the liaison between Allied Dunbar's Purchasing Department and other purchasing functions both inside and outside of financial services.

Geoff Winn is Senior Buyer and moved into purchasing from the print industry in 1976. His original role of Print Buyer has extended to working within various divisions of Allied Dunbar on contracts ranging from private medical care to micro computers. During the past four years the majority of his time has been spent providing purchasing support in the acquisition of software, hardware and telecommunications.

Alistair Haney is Distribution Services Manager. Since graduating in Business Administration from the University of Strathclyde in 1983, he has held various purchasing positions in the manufacturing and financial services sectors. He now has responsibility for warehousing and distribution and is working closely with the purchasing team to implement a materials management philosophy.

Acknowledgement

This book could never have been produced without a number of key players, all of whom made a significant contribution to both the book and the enjoyment of its production. In particular, thanks are extended to David Vessey, Clifford Green, Stewart Chapman, Lesley Baker, Chris Walker, Sara Hart and Kate Wilson.

CONTENTS

Foreword David L. Sheridan
Preface

1 Introduction	15
Purchasing opportunities	15
Traditional views of purchasing	17
Purchasing is about profit	20
Who judges purchasing success?	21
Summary	23
2 Proactive Purchasing – the Project Approach	25
Why be different?	25
Be proactive	29
Sell your strengths and skills	31
Use other people's strengths – project teams	32
Management of project purchasing	34
Checklist	38
3 Principles of Project Purchasing	39
Principles	39
Controls	41
Professional standards and ethics	43
Checklist	47
4 Dealing with Suppliers	49
Working with suppliers	49
Supplier selection	53
Supplier vetting	56
Supplier performance	59
Checklist	64

5 Negotiation — 65
- The objective of negotiation — 65
- Methods and techniques — 66
- Preparing for negotiation — 66
- Principles of negotiation — 71
- Assumptions — 74
- Tying up loose ends — 77
- Checklist — 80

6 Contracts — 81
- Model contracts — 82
- Liaison with the lawyers — 84
- Liaison with the audit department — 85
- Contract compilation — 86
- Building a contract library — 87
- Conclusion — 91
- Checklist — 92

7 Quality in Purchasing — 93
- What is quality? — 93
- Why is quality important? — 94
- Improving quality — 96
- Measurement — 97
- Savings — 99
- Feedback — 101
- Checklist — 103

8 Environmental Issues — 105
- Sources of information — 105
- Why is environment important? — 107
- Your contribution — 107
- Checklist — 110

9 Training and Development — 111
- Where to start — 111
- Training needs — 112
- Planning — 112
- Reinvesting the techniques — 113
- Team building — 114
- Checklist — 117

10 Consultancy within the Organisation   119
   Gaining entry   119
   Contracting   122
   Choosing a style   122
   Data gathering and problem identification   125
   Disengagement   126
   The ultimate client   128
   Checklist   129

11 Tips for Small Suppliers   131
   Small Business Enterprises   131
   Approaching large companies   132
   Professionalism   135
   A final word of encouragement   137

   Index   139

FOREWORD

During the last ten years or so, the purchasing function has tended to become increasingly fragmented in its objectives in an effort to find an acceptable and influential operational niche in corporate affairs. Thus, specialism has been surrendered to generality, while functional identity (which purchasing has always had some problems in establishing) has slipped even further out of focus. The result has been an uneasy and often acrimonious relationship with those in other disciplines.

Readers of this book will be relieved to find that it lacks any trace of pomposity or pretentiousness. It describes admirably the *commercial and contractual* role of purchasing, avoiding those flights of functional fancy likely to carry readers into alien and hostile territory in which no would-be top purchasing executive is likely to survive for long.

I understand that the purported purpose of this book was to illustrate how to position purchasing profitably in commercial and financial business sectors rather than in manufacturing industry. If so, the authors have been unnecessarily modest in their aspirations. Readers will find that the purchasing philosophy and principles expounded here are equally effective in *any* business context.

Despite the often vigorous activity to try to put purchasing 'on the map', the energy dissipated by those eventually discovering from the poor results that the wrong route has been selected gives cause for concern. This book avoids that, by pointing via commonsense and practicality the way towards purchasing responsibilities, authority and objectives that are workable, more readily acceptable to other functions and, above all, effective.

I commend the work to those seeking to find the 'right' path, as well as to those wanting confirmation that they are already on it.

David L. Sheridan F INST PS
Purchasing consultant and lecturer
Toad Hall, East Farleigh, Kent
January 1992

David Sheridan is a renowned international lecturer, writer and consultant and a Fellow of the Institute of Purchasing and Supply. Over a long and highly successful career he has held many key positions in both purchasing and sales. His monthly articles have been published for over twenty-five years in leading business journals.

PREFACE

In any company there are opportunities for professional buyers to make an impact and to add to company profit. To achieve this you have to grasp the fact that purchasing is not just about buying stationery, office equipment and furniture. The purchasing department's expertise needs to be focused on sound commercial activities rather than the specialisation of products. Only in this way will purchasing demonstrate its business value and improve its standing in the professional market.

This book is not merely for large, major purchasers. The principles voiced here are as valid for smaller companies, who will recognise the merits of an effective purchasing function that can add profit to the organisation.

If you have the opportunity to begin with a brand new operation you will quickly reap the benefits of better buying, while companies that already have purchasing departments steeped in years of doing the same thing will find in this book refreshing opportunities to make improvements in their own purchasing performance.

1
INTRODUCTION

This book is *not* an attempt to justify the existence of a professional purchasing function – that is taken for granted; nor does it deal with jargonistic aspects such as Just-in-Time, Materials Management, Logistics, etc., or bamboozle you with figures, graphs, formulae that make your hair stand up, or case studies of huge American or Japanese corporations wielding global pulling power.

This book concentrates instead on the basics of how purchasing should function, and how the effectiveness of the function can be visibly improved in many organisations. It tries to be as practical as possible and deliberately avoids presenting information in an 'academic' format, preferring to rely on the authors' personal experiences of purchasing in a wide range of organisations.

Purchasing opportunities

The current economic climate is arguably the best opportunity for any buyer worth his salt to make money for his company. You could consider that tough times leave all suppliers vulnerable to a killing from the wily negotiator, whereas during a boom the reverse opportunities for suppliers should prevail. This consideration is flawed, however. Purchasing people with money management in mind should be aware that there are as many opportunities in boom times as there are when recession begins to bite. It is our job to explore

ARE YOU MANAGING PURCHASING?

Traditional view of purchasing

all of the market changes to maximise profit for our companies.

To manage purchasing effectively, you need to be clear about what you are trying to achieve in terms of objectives and goals. One of your goals *must* be to make constant improvements in your effectiveness, as individuals and as a team, in your contribution to your organisation's profits, and in your perceived value to your organisation. Only by adopting this positive approach, and *proactively* doing something about it, can you hope to take the function where you want it to be.

This book aims to present a series of steps and measures you can take which will raise your effectiveness and position purchasing as a strategic contributor to company profits rather than a low-level administration or supply-based function which reacts to other departments' requests.

If this interests you, then read on . . . .

Traditional views of purchasing

Many purchasing departments are, out of necessity, concerned with the supply of goods and services to other areas of their organisation – whether it be obtaining components and materials to 'feed' the production line, negotiating deals with contract cleaners, supplying office consumables or computer hardware, and so on. The emphasis tends to be on *getting* the goods and services, and, if you're lucky, limiting price increases.

This type of purchasing can be termed 'Product Purchasing'. It is basically fuelled by requisition requests to purchase goods or services, and can be seen as a reactive response to demands from within your company (internal clients).

This approach to purchasing is not 'wrong', but so much more can be achieved. For a start, product purchasing doesn't have to be totally reactive; for example, requisition data can be used to anticipate future requests. There are also benefits in such work in that it provides a good training ground for the basics of purchasing, developing both technical and interpersonal skills with clients and suppliers.

Training ground

The objectives of any training initiatives are to assist performance and to allow for individual development. There are a host of courses covering purchasing skills and understanding; when linked to on-the-job training, these provide a good foundation. In addition, you should consider the benefits of talking to your counterparts in similar companies, in order to learn from each other's experiences. Product purchasing will present numerous opportunities to practise and develop the essential skills of a buyer in a regulated and controlled environment.

Requisition data

Rather than just processing paper, you should adopt a method of retaining and developing the data you are processing. Such a database may already be available through a Purchase Order or Inventory Control system. Alternatively, you could use a computer software package to create your own database. Once you have collected a reasonable amount of data, step back and take an overview of the situation to identify common areas of supply, consolidate product types and bring this information together to improve your purchasing power. This approach will also buy you more time to think about the methods you could use to improve your job and the status of purchasing in your company. 'Knowledge is power', as the old adage says.

Skills

The requirements of the job are not confined to purchasing techniques. There are a number of other skills to develop if you are to foster a good working relationship with both client and supplier. Consider where you and your team are in using the following skills:

- persuasion
- assertiveness
- communication
- telephone manner
- negotiation
- listening
- asking open questions
- meeting targets.

How could these skills be improved to demonstrate that purchasing has something more to offer than just administrative support? The list here is not exhaustive. There will be other skills peculiar to your own business environment which need developing.

Rounding-off the job

You may consider that placing an order concludes the business – it does not. A successful conclusion to any purchase will cover the quality issues of delivering on time, to the correct location, with the correct delivery paperwork; followed by correct invoicing and the timely payment of those invoices. Client feedback rounds off the job.

In addition, you may feel the need to expedite deliveries; but is this really necessary? If you have developed a quality working relationship with your suppliers, then you will achieve zero defects, deliveries on time, and correct paperwork. If not, then you will have been informed of problems in advance by your suppliers, which enables you to brief your client. In the real world, however, this often doesn't happen and you have to ask yourself why?

The costs to your company and to purchasing's reputation of not getting things right (thus adding cost instead of adding value) are potentially enormous and, until purchasing departments realise their true forte and begin to make things happen with their suppliers and clients, purchasing will be viewed as a low-level activity.

Remember, there are those who make things happen, there are those who watch things happen and there are those who wonder what the hell is happening! Into which category would you say your current purchasing activities fall? Anything less than the first category is not good enough.

Purchasing is about profit

How then do you develop from a product-based purchasing function driven by an endless stream of requisitions to a proactive, well-respected, professional buying function?

You should recognise that buying consists of two distinct sets of activities – those that are essentially administrative and clerical, and those that require purchasing skills. By segregating the work in this way, and accepting that different skills are required, it is quite logical to see that your purchasing department could be split into an 'order processing' operation and a 'project purchasing' function.

Using this style of approach, the order processing function will take responsibility for the administrative and added-cost activities of purchasing. This leaves the project purchasing operation free to concentrate on value-added activities.

By adopting this strategy you will find that you have the opportunity to demonstrate that your project purchasing team deals not in costs but rather in profits and can also influence events in the order processing area. That is to say, the members of the project purchasing team are no longer directly connected to the paperwork processors and are now 'free agents', able to operate on behalf of the client.

Who judges purchasing success?

It could be argued that there are two judges of purchasing success. One is the immediate client (the budget holder), who would be looking for benefits, say on a parochial basis, for his own (or departmental) activities. He may therefore be averse to some of the more commonsense suggestions that purchasing may wish to put forward.

The other judge is the company, which will be looking at overall effectiveness. The company will be concerned with the true saving in negotiation (money retained rather than money spent) and, instead of parochial 'nice to have' specifications purchased at best prices, will be looking at 'must have' areas and questioning more closely the total value of a product or service requested.

You will see that purchasing could be in a position of serving two masters: professionally we should be overseeing the total spend/total value on behalf of the company and influencing the local client to make the right company decisions, almost as much as influencing the supplier to come up with the right goods. Now you may be somewhat uncomfortable with the thought of serving two masters. You may feel that there is plenty of scope for conflict to arise between you and your local

ARE YOU MANAGING PURCHASING?

client if you are not wholeheartedly on your local client's side. You may even feel machiavellian.

However, this need not be the case. The following chapters will show how to organise, practise and perfect the professional purchasing function you have always longed for.

INTRODUCTION

Summary

- Purchasing does *not* need to be totally driven by requisitions from other departments.

- Training assists performance and development.

- Many tasks can be automated and separated from the entrepreneurial areas of purchasing.

- Purchasing is about adding value, not about cost.

2
PROACTIVE PURCHASING – THE PROJECT APPROACH

If you are competent at your purchasing job you should be able to buy better than anyone else in your organisation. If members of other departments continue to buy when there is a buying department, then it is either because you lack the required degree of competence, or because you have failed to convince clients that you can do the job better.

The usual solution to this is to seek a mandate from senior management insisting that only the purchasing department is authorised to commit expenditure to suppliers. However, this approach deals only with the symptoms of the problem, and often increases the tension between buyers and potential clients, which may subsequently develop into an adversarial relationship.

Why be different?

Why stick your neck out? ... Because purchasing has a major role to play in increasing the profitability of your company. Rather than operating predominantly as an administration department, providing little more than an ordering point for goods and services, you must demonstrate that you have a vehicle which is unique within the organisation, is proactive and clearly brings benefits to its clients. Such a purchasing function will:

- have clear goals and objectives
- be active in selling to your clients
- provide opportunities through invitation (not by mandate) for buyers to work across the company in multi-disciplined project teams
- cover every area of expenditure because the approach is money based rather than product specialised
- be performance related and look for project effectiveness in terms of added-value
- provide opportunities for your staff to develop as they work company-wide gaining a thorough understanding of the project, people and culture.

Everyone's a buyer

The danger of not having a strong purchasing focus is that the door becomes open to administrators who believe they can do an equal or better job.

For instance, you will have a variety of disciplines negotiating to spend company money:

Accounts:	bank charges, audit fees
Marketing:	advertising budgets, accommodation costs, conventions costs, print
Personnel:	medical insurance, consultancy fees, training fees, photocopying
Systems:	computer hardware, software licences
Office Services:	building maintenance, cleaning, security, catering.

Very few of these people will have any developed skill in commercial and contractual practice. They spend company money and they create contractual vulnerabilities.

It is not necessarily the client's fault. It is purchasing's responsibility to demonstrate its skills to the point where the client recognises the benefits that can be achieved by working with a skilled professional buyer. Failure to do this will mean that a greater percentage of company expenditure will continue to be committed outside the influence of the purchasing department.

As an exercise you might like to examine your current involvement against the overall company expenditure and begin to draw your own conclusions. No matter how large or small your company may be, a good purchasing department will have involvement in total company expenditure. Nothing is sacrosanct – involvement should cover areas such as bank charges, medical insurance, computer software licences, audit fees, solicitors' fees, consultancy costs.

Check out your accounts department invoice payments in their nominal ledger; you'll be surprised who's spending what and with whom! Armed with this information, you can start tackling these areas of expenditure on a project basis rather than waiting for the next contract renewal dates to arrive.

This style will produce a very positive approach within your department. The buyers should develop a successful marketing approach to project purchasing and back this up with a professional purchasing operation. The focus of almost everything you do is to influence the profitability of your company, while at the same time enhancing the reputation of purchasing.

Client satisfaction

Project purchasing departments work for clients or customers. If you are to attain credibility and status, you have to provide the client with a level of service better than they can achieve themselves... consistently.

To do this, purchasing has to be seen to specialise, not in administration and order processing but in the areas of commercial and contractual business. Your best weapon here is to expose your clients to your wide knowledge of:

- supplier sourcing/selection, to optimise the supply base
- company evaluation, to establish the financial standing of potential suppliers
- market forces, which may have an impact on the business
- negotiation techniques, to maximise the full benefits for your company
- interest rate awareness
- communication skills, to keep everyone up to speed on the project
- consultancy skills, to best develop working relationships
- sensitivity, to both the project and the personnel involved
- contract compilation, to ensure you use your own contracts rather than the supplier's
- contract reviews, to anticipate future needs before existing agreements expire.

Equally important, and therefore not to be overlooked, is the element of common sense. The client can sometimes get too close to the work. Purchasing's role here is to pick up the less obvious issues (issues such as competition, make or buy solutions, etc.) and develop them as ideas with the client. In addition, the client's approach may be too parochial, whereas purchasing should be taking a wider company view. Again, fresh ideas and a new approach to old problems could pay dividends in increasing purchasing's credibility.

Be proactive

By definition, if purchasing is to be proactive, then this must mean making suggestions and presenting ideas to clients *before* they make a decision to purchase. How can this be possible? Where is the purchasing crystal ball?

The key here is to go back to that nominal ledger in Accounts. Analysis of your company's total expenditure will put you in a position to identify a number of projects and approach clients with ideas about saving money, improving service levels, contractually safeguarding the company, etc. You will need to:

- check out the existing supplier's financial viability via a financial information service
- look for the competition within the product or service in question
- highlight the terms and conditions which are onerous within the contract or provide a draft contract of your own if there isn't one in existence
- suggest a negotiation strategy ready for the review date
- offer to meet your client and discuss your team's approach to purchasing and how you can help him.

This will provide the client with food for thought and may generate a review of the product or service in question or at least secure an invitation to be involved at an earlier stage next time round. You have now started the proactive approach.

Early involvement

Being proactive rather than reactive is one of the key elements in working with a project approach to purchasing.

To achieve this you need to be involved early in the decision-making stage of any expenditure.

The aim is to be invited into the project. Initially you could be in a position where you need to build client confidence about your abilities to add value. Talking with your client about his plans (budgets) for the year helps to begin to build a picture of his requirements. You then need to take up opportunities to explore his particular market of expenditure, discuss a strategy to help your client with your team, and communicate the ideas with him. It is also important to demonstrate to the client the success you've achieved in other areas.

There are a number of benefits to be achieved by obtaining early involvement. The greatest of these is **resource allocation**. In general, purchasing departments are relatively small in size and there is nothing worse than telling a client that purchasing will give support if none is available at the very time it is required. Especially in smaller companies where the principles of project purchasing still hold true, the purchasing resource will be smaller still, possibly just one person. So, scheduling your resource (which might just mean scheduling yourself) will be very important.

Other benefits of early involvement are:

- you can set out your role and how you will go about supporting the project at an early stage
- you can begin to get the feel of the sensitive issues within the project which may have an impact on future negotiations
- you will have an in-depth knowledge of the decision-making process involved in purchasing the product or service
- you can influence the removal of assumptions which are a barrier to effective purchasing
- you can prepare in advance for supplier selection and supplier appraisal exercises.

Pre-planning

Having persuaded your client to invite you into the project it would be a catastrophe if purchasing didn't perform (you may only get one chance). The skill here is to pre-plan both the approach to project meetings and the project role you are going to fulfil. Some of the considerations here are:

- Who are the other members of the team and what is their style of operation?
- Are you clear on the objectives and the end-result required?
- Do you understand what you're there for – commercial advice, contract advice, total control over the negotiation?
- Will the project be effective use of your time (how long will you be involved, what is the potential return)?
- Has the team got a supplier or suppliers already in mind?
- What assumptions are being made which will, if not removed, provide a barrier to the success of the project?

Remember: pre-plan your personal approach, probably by talking it through with colleagues, staff or other purchasing members. Then hold a pre-meeting with your client to ensure you know precisely what he is expecting from you and from the meeting.

Sell your strengths and skills

One of the skills you will need is the ability to market yourself and the project purchasing approach. No-one is going to come rushing to the purchasing door. You have to prove consistently that you can offer a better professional service than your client can achieve himself. To do this, consider the following:

- produce a purchasing brochure which sets out clearly the objectives, standards and ethics you and your team will meet
- gain an endorsement from the chief executive
- meet your clients, discuss and agree a future approach – some will welcome your approach, others will have nothing to do with it; develop those clients who want to work with you first
- keep in close contact with your clients, tell them what you're doing, tell them about the successes
- develop your ideas with senior management on a face-to-face basis, make them feel part of your decision-making process
- tell senior management what you're doing, explain your aims and goals, present key skills, discuss all the benefits and tell them about your successes.

If you don't understand what you're good at, it makes the selling of key skills extremely difficult. You need to work hard within your team to draw out the key attributes that you can successfully work with. In this area you may need professional training advice either from within your own organisation or using outside resource.

If you don't sell your skills within your company then you're leaving the purchasing initiatives to others and you will fail to make an impact.

Use other people's strengths – project teams

The worst thing a buyer can do is to try to be a 'Jack of all trades'. Project purchasing sets out to concentrate on commercial and contractual issues only and is heavily dependent on being able to obtain and use the skills of other people by working with them.

Probably the best approach to this is to construct a project team consisting of some or all of the following:

- the user (the person who actually operates the product or utilises the service; he will most probably be your client)
- the technical expert (generally the specifier of the product or service)
- the purchasing representative (you)
- the financial expert (to support viability, costs and cost models)
- the internal auditor (to ensure correct audit trails are in place)
- the legal expert (to ensure that particularly complex deals are supported).

There are no hard and fast rules about who it is best to have on a project team – you'll probably never get everyone together at once anyway! However, in any place of work you must always work with the user – never in isolation. The benefit of being in a smaller company is that people may represent more than one function – user and technical expert; financial expert and auditor.

It is not necessary for you to lead or chair the project team. In fact, it is probably best to avoid this role, which will give you the chance to concentrate on the key areas of negotiation and contracts. You can also act as a useful 'commonsense' foil for the group, as well as bringing your professional presence to bear. The best chairman will probably be the ultimate user of the goods or services ... after all, he is the real buyer, although he is using your professional skills.

Management of project purchasing

Within the project purchasing role there are opportunities to manage the project without actually chairing the group. By assertively stating purchasing's role and the expectations you have from the other team members you can quickly make an impact and gain agreement on the commonsense issues which are a major part of purchasing's brief; for example:

- the importance of lead times and the information you need to hit target dates
- the sensitivity of the product or service to the business
- the issues of confidentiality and strategy, which are key in a well-managed project.

With project purchasing, it is essential to maintain an enthusiastic, self-motivated team possessing all the required skills. It's not difficult to do; here are some ideas to consider.

Project variety

The project purchasing role moves buyers away from specialising in areas such as print, cars, stationery, office equipment, furniture, computers, etc. and into the arena of money management. Here you are concerned with profit and contractual safety for your company.

Rather than specialising in a product, buyers can be allowed to specialise within departments or divisions of an organisation, picking up all the purchasing initiatives from within those areas. They automatically become part of the departmental team, the 'purchasing expert', who can build a rapport through reputation based on successful purchasing projects. In this way, the need to sell the purchasing function reduces because the buyer is continually being invited to take a key role in expenditure.

This approach provides the opportunity to look at purchasing effectiveness with the client manager/director and agree which areas of expenditure need high-level purchasing input and which areas need purchasing advice and coaching.

Strengths and weaknesses

Before you or one of your buyers starts to work with a particular department or area of the business you will need to have an understanding of the skills you possess and where limitations exist. You will also need to understand the requirements of the department so that you can match up the resource. For instance, a marketing area will have totally different staff from, say, an accounts area.

Obviously these considerations will become of prime importance when you are recruiting purchasing staff. The correct mix will provide you with a very powerful team indeed, able to work anywhere within your organisation.

Team spirit

Maintain a good team spirit through regular meetings; half an hour first thing in the morning is a good time to share successes and failures amongst the buyers and to discuss issues. Perhaps a negotiation didn't go as well as planned – talking about it may reveal why.

Using other buyers as sounding boards for ideas tends to spark greater ideas – two heads are better than one! If you *are* the purchasing department, then find someone to whom you can relate and confide; someone you can rely on for an honest opinion.

Twinning

Salesmen rarely hunt alone! Yet for some reason buyers feel capable of tackling two or perhaps three well-trained salesmen on their own. This is nonsense! If it is an important meeting with a lot of money at stake then use two or even more buyers in conjunction with the client and agree beforehand what each person's role and objectives will be.

In very large companies you may even include an extra buyer in a meeting with the sole intention of providing feedback on his colleagues' performance. There is great value in this, especially as you each strive to improve your effectiveness.

Rotation

If buyers are 'allocated' to specific clients, and are used to dealing in a particular area(s), it is worthwhile swapping round every now and then. This has the benefit of bringing a fresh pair of eyes into an area and will also introduce a spirit of competition amongst buyers, who will try to outdo each other's deals!

If buyers are rotated, it must be done with the willingness and co-operation of their clients, and should be treated sensitively. A careful balance between consistency and variety needs to be struck.

Control and effectiveness

There are a number of areas within the purchasing function which enable you to test the effectiveness of the project team:

- measuring savings generated against the actual salaries and related overhead costs of the purchasing team – if you were running a commercial business you would expect this equation to show a profit
- quantifying the value of additional contractual protection secured by the purchasing function, compared with the cost of doing the work
- asking the client for feedback on the latest piece of work you have undertaken, listening to his views and showing continuous improvement
- comparing quality improvements and/or cost savings in the client's department with the costs of achieving these results.

The greatest measure of effectiveness is when the client makes the first approach and invites purchasing into the project team.

Checklist

- Focus on purchasing's influence on the profitability of the company. Don't devalue the function.

- Recognise that purchasing's forte is commercial and contractual business.

- Market purchasing to clients.

- Purchasing departments work for clients/customers, so you must provide better than the client can achieve.

- Be proactive in project purchasing.

- Get purchasing involved early in projects.

- Use other people's expertise.

- Develop a team which is professional, competitive and whose members 'feed off' each other.

3
PRINCIPLES OF PROJECT PURCHASING

Project purchasing is an entrepreneurial approach to purchasing but this does not mean that it should have any less discipline or fewer principles than any other form of organised buying.

Principles

You will need a set of rules to establish and maintain standards (there is also a value in publishing them within your company). The following embody an approach to good purchasing practice:

- Always abide by the spirit and letter of the law.
- Observe a code of conduct and ethics.
- Strive for professionalism at all times. Aim to be seen by suppliers as firm but fair and a customer with whom they want to deal.
- Always seek to introduce competition.
- Base your decision to purchase on thorough supplier evaluation, analysis and negotiation. This ensures that the optimum balance of price, quality and supply arrangements is achieved.

ARE YOU MANAGING PURCHASING?

Observe a code of conduct and ethics

- Business should always be placed with the best supplier.
- Suppliers should always be evaluated to ensure that they are sound organisations that can supply the quantity and quality required for as long as the service is needed.
- Consider the impact of taking up a major part of a supplier's production or service capacity. Strike a balance between being a large enough customer to warrant good service, but not so big as to make suppliers vulnerable to the withdrawal of business or vice versa.
- Continually review supply arrangements for goods and services to ensure best value for money.
- Always honour agreements with suppliers (verbal or written), unless a supplier's action invalidates any previous agreement.
- Ensure written agreements or contracts are always established with suppliers.
- Provide a sound audit trail for all purchases to reduce the opportunity for fraudulent activity.

Controls

Project purchasing must operate in an environment which is well controlled and operates to rigorous standards and audit requirements.

In the majority of companies there is a requirement to raise paperwork for the placing and processing of purchasing orders. This could include documents such as requisitions, purchase orders, call-off orders on standing contracts, contracts and working agreements. Other paperwork processed locally will include delivery notes, order confirmations, invoices and acknowledgements.

While there may be a need for separate ordering systems, you should ensure that each of them meets the objectives and guidelines set out in your purchasing approach, the requirements of internal and external auditors, the quality standards in dealing with suppliers, and the authority limits set by your company. Your company will then have some protection against potential fraudulent practice.

To add to the quality of your department's controls, you need to ensure that four main 'good practice' requirements are observed:

- the correct paperwork sequence
- an audit trail
- evidence of supplier competition
- clearly defined authority limits.

These are covered in more detail below.

Paperwork sequence

The sequence of events in placing a purchase order and subsequent authorising of payment needs to be logical. For instance, raising a purchase order after receipt of the supplier's invoice should be an unacceptable practice.

Audit trail

You should ensure that there is always a well-defined, traceable audit trail containing authorisation by more than one person between critical points of the paperwork:

- raising a requisition
- authorising the requisition
- raising/signing the purchase order
- signing for delivery/completion
- authorising the payment.

There should never be consecutive signing by the same person during the five stages.

Supplier competition

It is good purchasing practice to show evidence that alternative suppliers have been considered for the business. Alternative quotations, estimates and analysis should be kept, with backup correspondence showing the reasons for selecting suppliers.

Authority limits

In dealings with suppliers, care should be taken not to exceed internal authority limits. Commitments can be legally enforceable against your company, even in cases where an employee does not have specified internal authority.

Professional standards and ethics

The principles of purchasing ethics can be emotive topics, with different views being offered across any company about the acceptability or unacceptability of the approach. Clearly a marketing department will have a different view for instance on gifts and incentives than your own purchasing department.

What you have to do is agree an approach with your purchasing team, then maintain it consistently. Again, it helps to publish what you have decided across your company.

The stand you make and the consistency of approach are important considerations in the professionalism of your department. In recent years the press has been full of instances where purchasing people have let their profession down because of unethical practice. You owe it to yourself and to your company to display professionalism beyond question or doubt.

Some of the areas which could be covered in a code of conduct are discussed below.

Confidentiality

Most discussions with suppliers, or potential suppliers, will involve information of a confidential nature. The confidentiality and sensitivity of this information should be respected at all times.

Suppliers will often ask you to keep special trading arrangements confidential. Their position in the market place will be weakened if you reveal, for instance, discount levels, production schedules or special delivery arrangements. This type of confidentiality should always be honoured.

Confidentiality is particularly relevant when dealing with project teams and it is valuable to emphasise the point within these teams.

Alternatively, you may be in the position of having to release confidential information to a supplier in order for them to be able to quote for business or complete a contract. Confidential data should only be released if they are absolutely necessary and the supplier is made aware of the consequences of any breach of this trust.

Remember your professional reputation is at risk if you abuse confidential agreements.

Incentives and entertainment

A lot of suppliers still offer gifts or incentives to customers, either for business placed or, in some cases, for potential business. Gifts can include lunches, event tickets and social functions. This is a very sensitive area and one where you should take a commonsense approach with all suppliers at all levels to avoid compromising your position.

Consider making it a policy that:

- Your team will not accept gifts or entertainment from any contractor/supplier with whom you do not deal. Agree to decline politely if such offers are made.
- Your team will not accept an incentive from any contractor/supplier with whom you do deal. Again, in such cases agree to decline politely. *However*, lunch is often part of a sales presentation or seminar and in some cases you may agree that this could be accepted as part of the business relationship, but consider it within the bounds of common sense.
- Any business entertainment received by yourself from a contractor/supplier should be openly declared. In this respect, *any* entertainment received should be identified and acknowledged with a personal letter of thanks which is then kept on file.
- In some instances, it may be worth reciprocating and contributing your share of expenses for the provision of lunch.
- When you do entertain a contractor/supplier, it should be to further the working relationship to the benefit of your company.

Personal interests

You should agree that anyone involved in purchasing should always represent your company's best interests.

If at any time when dealing with suppliers or potential suppliers, anyone should have a personal, business or family connection, this should be declared immediately. Equally, any interest which might be construed as prejudicing good business relationships should always be declared. In order to protect both the person and your company from potential embarrassment or conflict of interest it will be worthwhile leaving the individual out of that particular business arena.

Personal conduct

When dealing with suppliers you are representing your company, so it is important that all dealings reflect your company's high standards. The issues here include attitude to suppliers, punctuality, quality of response, meeting agreed targets and a courteous approach.

It is also important to demonstrate professionalism and a high quality of work from initial contact, through negotiation and agreement to supply.

It should be your responsibility to ensure that all transactions with suppliers are clear, unambiguous and honoured in full, unless terminated or modified by mutual consent. You should also ensure that your company is not committed to agreements that cannot be fulfilled.

Checklist

- Work to and publish your set of purchasing rules.

- Maintain purchasing controls:
  - follow correct paperwork sequence
  - keep to an audit trail
  - provide evidence of supplier competition
  - work within authority limits.

- Agree an approach to purchasing ethics, publish it and be consistent.

- Respect supplier confidentiality.

- Maintain your professional reputation.

- Take a commonsense approach to gifts and incentives.

- Watch out for personal interest, and see it is declared.

- Maintain high standards of personal conduct.

4
DEALING WITH SUPPLIERS

Dealing with suppliers is one of the key purchasing functions. The way you and your company go about this plays an important part in establishing the professionalism of the purchasing function, the credibility of individuals and the reputation of your company.

It is worth stating that in business the 'wheel of fortune' always turns full circle: where we haven't been professional, credible or enhanced our reputation, those areas have a tendency to return and haunt us. For instance: how many times have hasty assumptions or poor preparation caused you to produce a service which did not fully meet your client's needs – leading to them not willingly asking you back again?

Similarly, if you do not meet suppliers on time and do not treat them in a courteous fashion, why be surprised when they supply you in a like manner?

Working with suppliers

The amount of effort that is placed on working with suppliers should be relative to the value and sensitivity of the business to be placed. Additionally, you should consider whether you are placing a once-off contract, following which the relationship will end, or whether the contract is the start of a long-term relationship. Of course, the supplier must be able to meet your contract and client needs.

The following pointers provide some of the key 'good practices' for working with suppliers.

Credibility

It is essential to maintain credibility with a supplier.

Supplier relationships should always be handled in a fair and ethical manner (see later chapters). Lost credibility through leaking confidences, providing inaccurate information, and empty threats will take a long time to recover, if at all.

Never misrepresent the business to improve deals, disclose a supplier's information to the competition, or make threats or promises that cannot be upheld or are outside your authority.

It is important that the supplier sees you as having the authority to make decisions. If a supplier feels he is dealing with a 'middle man', he will be far less attentive to your requests (think about how you feel when a supplier has continually to refer to a higher authority for a decision).

Proactive approach

Be proactive and consider future developments that may affect your supplier's welfare or business.

Don't surprise a supplier with events that directly affect his business. If you know business volumes are going to reduce, tell him in plenty of time. Alternatively, if volumes are going to increase, tell him so that any necessary preparations can be made. He will then be in a better position to meet your needs.

Meeting terms

Each element of an agreed deal is subject to you and the supplier meeting the terms of your agreement. For example, continually paying a supplier later than agreed is indefensible. If the supplier's money is late in arriving, why should he feel that your next order should be delivered on time?

As the person negotiating the terms you are responsible for ensuring that all parties involved meet their obligations. It is therefore essential never to agree to terms that are outside your control without obtaining agreement from the relevant area.

Expediting

Expediting is a means of progressing work in hand with a supplier to ensure that agreed delivery schedules are met or amended should the need arise.

There are various views, indeed whole books, on expediting, mainly covering whether it is or is not necessary. Generally, if a deal has been agreed and each party meets their obligations, then expediting should not be necessary. Indeed, you could argue that it only adds cost to the overall process.

In some areas of purchasing, the expediting role is seen as a necessary part of a process to control a flow of material and to know when contingencies are required should the flow be interrupted. A non-expediting approach can be achieved if these issues are built into contractual agreements.

However, where suppliers are providing goods which can be affected by bad weather (e.g. perishable foods or long-distance imports), it may still be necessary to check that all is well.

If any problems arise, a good supplier will contact you

ARE YOU MANAGING PURCHASING?

Supplier selection: complacency and laziness

immediately so that necessary actions can be discussed with you. For significant goods or services you will already have discussed and agreed contingency plans for just this turn of events.

Supplier selection

Purchasing's success comes through working well with both clients and suppliers. The client will need comfort, consideration and communication. On the supplier side, an aggressive approach to sourcing and selection is essential. It is important constantly to seek new sources of supply and to use a healthy competitive approach to your company's advantage.

Complacency and laziness will take you down the same old supply route, which only succeeds in reducing purchasing's effectiveness in the market place. Although there are benefits from a regular supplier who knows your requirements very well and with whom you have built a good working relationship, this should never remove the process of regular marketplace and supplier checks to ensure that the best value is always being obtained for your company.

Here are a number of considerations which help this approach:

- trawl the market in a professional manner, sending suppliers a detailed questionnaire on themselves and the services they provide
- remove the 'three quotes' barrier by giving everyone in the field an opportunity to respond
- concentrate on the quality aspects of performance (product, paperwork, delivery standards)
- provide suppliers with information on your own company
- give suppliers a set amount of time in which to respond

- investigate individual supplier trading viability through a recognised agency (Dun & Bradstreet), with a database (Infolink), maybe via your own in-house micro
- analyse the information they provide and the way they provide it, and categorise the suppliers
- let suppliers know if they have been successful (shortlisted) or have failed to impress
- remove assumptions about suppliers' abilities by testing them out, getting them to perform.

This approach should help you to source new areas of supply and keep existing suppliers aware that they can't afford to be complacent about your business. Listed below are the key stages of selecting a supplier and building a relationship which will ensure confidence that agreements will be met.

Initial contact

Once the specification of the product and/or service has been decided and the decision to purchase made, you can make initial contact with suppliers.

Your initial contact list can come from:

- your client's preferred suppliers
- a manufacturer dealer list
- literature specifically produced to list suppliers of products/services
- previously received introductory letters.

You should avoid making contact with suppliers with whom you have no intention of dealing. This can only extend the supplier selection exercise unnecessarily and lead to lack of enthusiasm during potential meetings.

You might consider not dealing with a supplier because of problems in the past, personality clashes, assumptions that they cannot meet your requirements, or negative feedback from other customers. These are all areas which might not necessarily be the fault of the supplier and by removing a supplier early in your selection process you may be missing a trick.

There should always be a solid commercial reason for removing a supplier from your initial contact list. You should not allow your client to make assumptions that a supplier is unsuitable.

Once the initial list has been agreed with your client, you can make contact with the suppliers. There are obviously various ways to do this – by telephone, in face-to-face meetings and in writing. The latter is preferable and more efficient at this stage.

Provide each supplier with an identical specification and list of questions. Not only does this ensure ease of supplier vetting when reading their responses, but fair treatment of all suppliers involved is seen by all concerned.

How many

There are no hard and fast rules on how many suppliers you should contact for an initial response. How many are available could be dictated by the type of product or service you intend to purchase; you could be in a single-source supply arena.

If the potential contract value is considerable and a long-term competitive contract is essential, then there is nothing stopping you making initial contact with twenty or more suppliers. However, despite high value and lengthy timescales this might not always be possible, for example when purchasing bank charges. Bear in mind, too, that you will need to vet each of the responses and you could be inundated with phone calls from suppliers. Also, a supplier can become demotivated if made aware that the competition is in double figures. You will have to use your best judgement when weighing these factors one against the other.

There will always be a concern that a supplier not contacted might be the right one for the job. By contacting a large number of suppliers initially you will have confidence that the supplier you ultimately select is the most suitable and competitive for the products and services you know you will need to buy in the near future. In the process, you will have gathered a lot of information that can aid you during negotiations and help with selecting different suppliers for new types of products if the need arises.

In all supplier dealings you need to take a commonsense approach to the level of contact. Obviously if your spend is below £5000 you may consider it prudent to develop, say, only two or three suppliers. If you're putting together a deal on print or stationery, you could trawl maybe ten suppliers if the value and sensitivity warranted it. As the spend increases you may in fact find that the supplier list diminishes (as with bank charges) because you would wish to involve only key suppliers.

In the end, only experience will provide you with the best guide to approaching suppliers and building supplier lists.

One last thought about this often very time-consuming process: do not lose sight of your own costs. You are there to *add* value to the business, so don't spend days tracking down that elusive supplier who is a pound cheaper than anyone else.

Supplier vetting

The time involved in vetting suppliers with the objective of selecting the right one can vary considerably. You may decide that the initial response to your specification is enough for you to make a decision. Alternatively you may decide that the duration, value and sensitivity of the contract, together with the requirements of your client, warrant a higher level of vetting.

What to look for

Does your contract require the provision of a product or service to your company over a considerable time period, say several years? If so, you need to be confident that the supplier will still be around. So ask yourself:

- What is the financial position of the supplier?
- What other contracts does he have?
- What are his plans for the future?
- Is he in a position that he could be bought/sold and what would the effect be on your contract?
- Does he rely on substantial support from a third party (i.e. manufacturer) and what if this support is withdrawn?
- What contingencies/disaster back up can the supplier provide?

You also need to know what effect your contract will have on the supplier and where you will be placed as a customer if your contract value is a high percentage of the supplier's turnover – will he be able to handle it? What if the supplier employs additional staff or invests in additional equipment if he obtains your contract? How will that affect him if you terminate or do not renew the contract?

Conversely, what if your potential contract value is a small percentage of the supplier's turnover? Will larger customers take priority?

If you intend to reduce your initial contacts down to a shortlist, you will need to consider how competitive they are, and to what degree each supplier is prepared to meet your contract terms and conditions. Does the supplier contractually guarantee his service level? How long will prices remain fixed and are there any hidden costs?

It may not be necessary, given the nature of the contract, to consider such lengthy criteria. It is always advisable to work with your client when creating a checklist for testing the sensitivity and value of a contract.

The client's needs

You should continually communicate with clients and consider their needs. While you may be able to see clear commercial reasons for the suppliers you are recommending, your clients may have their own views on some of those companies and perhaps different priorities from you. While these priorities should not take precedence over making commercial decisions, they should be addressed and made part of the vetting process.

Never forget that the client may have to work with the selected supplier for a long time after you have moved on to other things. It is therefore important that each stage is well documented and that you display a professional approach to the business at all times. The chosen supplier could also be one of your existing suppliers for another client (as could rejected suppliers), which places your professionalism into even greater focus. There is no harm in being hard when negotiating, while at the same time leaving the supplier feeling he has been fairly treated.

Shortlisting

Your 'shortlist' of suppliers may contain the same number as originally contacted, if they have all responded well, or a reduced number following supplier vetting and elimination. The shortlist should include those suppliers with whom you would be confident about entering into a contract. Meetings should then be arranged for the price and contract negotiations.

Your final chosen supplier should be the one offering the best 'value' to your client. This might not be the supplier offering the lowest price if, say, for this you will receive a product and service at the lowest end of the scale (e.g. barely meets the technical specification and can just about meet the delivery schedule). You and your client may prefer a supplier who, for just a slightly higher price, has a far more attractive product, readily available, etc. It is most important that your client understands the concept of good all-round value. Once a supplier agrees to a contract, then he really must meet it. The result should be a good product at a low price with good service.

Supplier performance

It is not safe to assume that once the contract is in place you can walk away confident that the original requirements will always be met.

Any number of things can contribute to a reduction or gradual deterioration in service from the supplier. As service is an important element for which you are paying, it therefore follows that the original deal is not being met. But how to measure that deterioration and prove your point is now the question.

Measurement

There are various methods for measuring supplier performance, but it all comes down to the consistency with which the supplier meets the terms of the contract. It is therefore essential that the original contract clearly defines the service level you require and the way in which that service will be measured.

The person best placed to monitor supplier performance is the client. Feedback should be encouraged and poor performance acted upon immediately. The feedback mechanism and an agreed period of review dates will provide you with the chance to build up a dialogue of continuity with your client. It will also help the development of future business.

It is important to do this soon after commencement of the contract so that a pattern of meetings and feedback reviews is quickly established as the way in which you wish to work. It is no good 'suffering in silence' and then holding an annual review meeting with the supplier at which you tell him for the first time that his service has been poor.

Measurement criteria

In providing a service there are a number of elements that can create measurement criteria:

- clear technical specification of required product
- accuracy and timeliness of delivery
- absence of complaints from clients/users
- how proactive the supplier is
- clear paperwork produced within an agreed number of days after delivery
- ability to resolve problems within specified time periods.

If specific criteria are identified against which to monitor performance, beware that they do not involve you or the client in a lot of unnecessary administration. Make your measurement benchmarks clear, simple and unambiguous.

Ideally you should identify a method that is self-measuring, can be checked with minimal effort and is immediately apparent to the client and reported directly to the supplier.

Reviews

Once you have passed the early days of a contract and the service is flowing as required, a good way of maintaining contact with a supplier is to hold regular review sessions. These could be quarterly or half-yearly, depending on the complexity of the contract, and should involve you, the client and obviously the supplier.

The regular meetings can provide an opportunity to review issues from the previous period, outline what is happening in your own company and discuss future plans and other business opportunities if applicable. You should then discuss cost-saving ideas that could work for both companies, negotiate the next contract period and identify any concerns the supplier may have.

An overall benefit of regular review sessions is that potential problem areas are identified before they become serious, while the supplier is directly motivated. You should aim to build a good working relationship where either you or the supplier would quickly contact each other should any problems arise.

Motivation

Everyone from time to time needs motivation and a supplier is no exception. The contractual provision of goods and services in return for your money may not be enough to keep a supplier enthusiastic and proactive.

There are two main factors that can provide motivation to an existing supplier:

- potential additional business
- the threat of losing existing business.

Additional business is not always on offer and the threat of taking business away can be used only once. So, what's left? Praise, gifts, lunches, etc. The long-term motivational value of these is doubtful.

A more effective method of motivating suppliers over the longer term is regular contact to discuss existing business and what is happening in your company. After all, your supplier is in business to do business, nothing else.

A few ideas that could add value to this process:

- Consider hosting a supplier seminar on your premises, bringing in the MD or marketing director to explain your company's approach/philosophy as well as adding the purchasing points you wish to get across. Provide lunch and a reasonable level of hospitality. Most importantly, be professional.
- Arrange an inter-company sporting event (cricket, football, squash) where people can mix socially and get to know one another outside of the working environment. This is particularly useful for long-standing suppliers.

Either of these will lead to the supplier feeling more part of the team, seeing additional business opportunities, but also feeling in sympathy with your company's objectives.

Addressing success/failure

It is as important to address a supplier's success as his failures. All too often you can jump on the failure and take success for granted.

If a supplier is successful in maintaining agreed service levels and this generates positive feedback from your client(s), he should be told this in order to show that this is the type of customer reaction you want to see. **Remember, good, poor or indifferent supplier performance will reflect upon you.**

If a supplier begins to fail in his obligations, look for reasons why this is happening. You may be able to help resolve the problems, given your now much wider role in the purchasing world.

Often the hardest part of a buyer's job is dealing with poor supplier performance. This may need instant action and an immediate change of supplier. However, with good initial supplier selection and a well-documented supply history, this should be rare.

If the matter cannot be resolved, then business to the suppliers should either be gradually reduced (if possible) and an alternative supplier brought on to supply the balance, or an instant break made. Whichever decision is taken, it should be done clearly and professionally, with no room for misunderstanding about the original problem or the action taken.

Checklist

- When working with suppliers be professional
  - never misrepresent your business
  - never disclose confidential information.

- Test out your assumptions.

- Meet all the obligations of your contract.

- If you're dealing with a quality supplier, why expedite?

- Constantly seek new sources of supply.

- Ensure that suppliers are thoroughly vetted.

- Consider what the client needs from a supplier.

- Measure supplier performance.

- Review each contract thoroughly.

- Provide supplier motivation to assist the business relationship.

5
NEGOTIATION

There are various definitions of negotiation, the majority based on people's perception rather than on the real meaning of negotiation.

Quite simply, the definition of negotiation is 'confer to reach an agreement'. It does not matter how long or how hard you negotiate. You have not completed or succeeded in a negotiation until agreement has been reached.

The objective of negotiation

Because agreement is essential to a successful negotiation, all negotiations have to be based on what is realistic and possible.

Agreement should not be confused with compromise, as in all negotiations you will be trying to obtain agreement on your requirements and not meeting a supplier half-way.

Win/win or win/lose

When entering a negotiation you will have an idea of the agreement you wish to reach. Unfortunately your preferred agreement may totally contradict that of the supplier with whom you are negotiating. This can lead to a trading of requirements which results in both parties settling on what they feel they set out to achieve. This is a win/win situation. Alternatively, either you or the supplier may, through negotiation, obtain agreement on all requirements without any concessions, while the other party does concede to reach agreement. This is a win/lose situation.

The vulnerability in adopting a win/win approach is that it begins to condition your mind to compromise, and these thoughts will ultimately stop you achieving your objectives because you will be prepared to give ground at the outset of a negotiation. Your overall objective is to secure agreement on the best deal you can, which means the supplier meeting all your requirements.

Methods and techniques

Methods and techniques of negotiation cover areas such as planning, tactics, psychology, strategy and manipulation.

Your first negotiation may be the start of many and it is essential that your supplier sees you as genuine. So you must ensure that you have the authority to make decisions, that you keep to your agreements and that you maintain a strictly ethical approach to business (don't be tempted to feather your own nest). It is important that negotiations never involve trickery, false promises, threats or anything that makes a supplier feel he has been misled.

Preparing for negotiation

Competition

In trying to achieve your objectives in negotiation, one of your most important strengths is the availability of competition. Competition should be actively encouraged, with suppliers being made aware that they are in a competitive situation.

It is amazing how the introduction of competition can create a dramatic change in service levels and price from an existing supplier. For instance, in 1990 a large household name company was notified by their longstanding maintenance contractors that a price increase would become effective on the next 1 January. Despite several years of good service from the supplier, the company's requirement was still put out to competitive bidding amongst the supplier's competitors. Although the company stayed with the original supplier, the exercise brought many improvements in the service provided, such as:

- better call-out times
- provision for an on-site engineer
- free maintenance periods
- reduction in cost of parts
- payment in arrears instead of in advance
- no price increase; in fact a reduction was achieved
- contract extension – say two years
- regular maintenance reports to the client
- quarterly instead of monthly invoices
- contract terms and conditions provided by the customer not the supplier
- prompt payment discounts.

Clearly the market had moved on since the original contract had been established with the supplier. What would have been unheard of some time ago was now commonplace amongst their competitors.

Remember, always check the competition and make sure that every supplier knows that is what you are doing.

Information gathering

Preparation and information gathering for a forthcoming negotiation are essential and will almost certainly take more time than the negotiation itself. Without the right amount of preparation and information you will not succeed in obtaining the best possible deal.

The sort of questions you should be asking are:

- What is the supplier's financial status – his profit margins and turnover?
- Comparing your likely expenditure with these figures, how important is your business?
- When does the supplier's financial year end? Will he make concessions to obtain your contract before a specific date?
- Will your company add an impressive name to the supplier's client list?
- Where is the supplier placed in the market? Does your business make him number one?
- Does the person you are about to negotiate with have the authority to agree to your requirements?
- Will your business generate a commission to a third party?

Setting objectives

You should set objectives for a negotiation as you would for any meeting, but it is important to avoid fixed targets. By identifying targets you are making assumptions which may turn out to be less than a supplier is prepared to give. It is far better to aim to maximise your deal through negotiation.

You must be clear on what you need to agree. If you are not, you will never know when agreement has been reached.

For instance, when dealing with the provision of hotel accommodation you will need management reports on take-up of accommodation, meals and services with an indication of the room rate, taking into account single and double rooms plus arrival and departure times. You will want to agree when payment has to be made (weekly, monthly, on account), looking for a retrospective rebate on turnover volume. You will want room services such as tea/coffee/flowers in the rooms plus conference/interview facilities. All this you will want to agree in a contract, using your own terms and conditions in what may be a national as well as a local agreement.

This list is by no means comprehensive, but provides some of the considerations which ought to precede a negotiation meeting to ensure that you emerge with everything your client requires.

Selecting the negotiating team

One more thing before entering the negotiating room. It is important that the right people attend the meeting.

You and your client will, in the majority of cases, be the only people necessary for a successful negotiation, especially if you have kept interested parties aware of progress. You may from time to time have a requirement for other skills, such as legal, audit, accounts and technical. However, too many people can be disruptive and make the supplier feel uneasy. You will find negotiating easier and more positive if you keep the number of people to a minimum.

Whoever attends must be thoroughly briefed. You should control the meeting, but it is essential that the rest of the team are aware of each other's roles. All negotiations benefit from a pre-meeting of the selected team, which gives you an opportunity to state what you want and don't want from the attendees. Remember not to criticise your colleagues during negotiation and don't

ARE YOU MANAGING PURCHASING?

Selecting the negotiating team

pretend that you have superior technical knowledge about the particular goods or services.

Principles of negotiation

Persuasion

There are five main aspects of persuasion which could be used during a negotiation:

(1) *Compromise*, which is quite often confused with the term 'negotiation' and is considered by many to be a fair way of reaching agreement. To compromise, however, *both* parties have to concede.

(2) *Bargaining*, where each party trades options to reach agreement. This give and take process does not, as with compromise, mean meeting half-way, but both parties will have to make concessions.

(3) *Coercion*, which is when a negotiator, coming from a position of (real or perceived) power, tries to force the other party into agreement.

(4) *Emotion*, which when controlled can provide considerable benefits in negotiation, especially when using statements such as:
'I need your help on . . .'
'I just can't get comfortable with . . .'
'Paying that amount will cause me problems with . . .'

(5) *Logical reasoning*, as a result of planning a well-structured, well-reasoned case. The negotiator can use logical reasoning to support their requirements while undermining the requirements of the other party.

Listening

During all negotiations it is important to listen. Don't let yourself be drawn into a situation where you are continually qualifying the reasons behind your requests. Don't let yourself diversify into areas that do not relate to the points under discussion.

If there are concessions to be made, the person talking the most will make the most!

Creating the atmosphere

Successful negotiations invariably start from a relaxed and friendly approach. You should move into a negotiation rather than dive in as soon as you are all sat down. The latter approach could make a supplier raise his guard and make him feel somewhat unwelcome.

If it is within your control, select an area for negotiation that is comfortable and free from interruption. You should be free from time constraints and at ease. In this situation you are less likely to concede during the negotiation.

Opportunities in negotiation

You should continually be aware of the opportunity to negotiate and maximise the benefits to your company. Don't be put off by comments such as, 'We did a really good deal last time' or 'They are the only supplier available'. Situations change.

You will automatically negotiate every time an offer is made. Negotiation could be accepting the offer as it stands, or putting the right amount of effort into reducing the negative impact of the offer.

What to negotiate

It is all too often thought that the negotiable element of a deal is cost and therefore this is what is concentrated on during negotiation.

Whilst cost is obviously important in any negotiation that involves a financial outlay, a considerable number of other areas (over seventy options) can show an advantage and benefit through negotiation; some of them are:

- price
- discounts – bulk
- preferred customer
- price stability
- price variation formula
- prices on sliding scale
- payment terms
- currency/exchange rate
- deferral of price increases
- delivery costs
- delivery dates
- delivery location(s)
- delivery frequency
- insurance
- quality and specification(s)
- quality confidence (new supplier)
- performance guarantees
- reliability
- free samples
- assistance with promotions/trials
- flexibility to changes
- consignment stock
- consolidated stock
- buffer stocks
- collection of rejects/surplus
- emergency response
- buy-back agreement
- lead time/availability
- maintenance/spares/call out.

Don't concentrate on the price and miss other areas which make a considerable difference to the overall total cost.

Knowing your supplier

Your supplier's motives for obtaining your business may not just be increased revenue.

Always be aware of your supplier's needs and priorities and consider these during your negotiations. The information you pulled together during your preparation for these negotiations should give you a powerful hand to play.

Assumptions

It is dangerous to make assumptions during negotiations. If you assume something, you are gambling that you are correct in your assumption. As in any form of gambling, from time to time you are going to be wrong.

Also, beware of other people – even so-called experts – trying to influence you with their assumptions. You will often hear these people say:

- 'The supplier will never accept these terms and conditions.'
- 'He's a good supplier, we've been dealing with them for twenty years.'
- '10 per cent is a reasonable price increase in the current climate.'
- 'We've got to let the supplier make a profit.'
- 'There's no way they'll meet these delivery schedules.'

No matter how obvious something may seem, different assumptions can be made by different people. Always test and challenge every aspect of a deal. Your supplier is going to be skilled at not offering you everything he could – so you must work at getting the best from him on every point throughout the negotiation.

Questioning

Question everything and don't make any assumptions based on your own knowledge. Question what you have read or been told and, if not absolutely clear, question it again.

Don't assume that because three suppliers do not charge for delivery neither does the fourth. Always ask the question and then negotiate on the answer until you have the answer your client needs.

Gaining understanding

During negotiations, continually give a supplier the opportunity to gain understanding and clarification. Irrespective of how well you feel you communicate, don't assume that people have understood you correctly. Always give your supplier the opportunity to feed back to you his understanding of your requests or requirements. It won't do you any good if he has misunderstood a point.

Summarising

Throughout negotiation, continually summarise the discussions, outline your understanding of what has been said and agreed so far, and give the supplier the opportunity to correct your understanding.

At the end of a negotiation summarise the entire agreement which has been reached.

Do's and Dont's in Negotiation

Do's

- *Preparation*
  Prepare for a negotiation according to the value and complexity of the potential contract. Look for all areas that can provide you with an advantage.
- *Aiming high*
  Set your objectives high, which will allow you to be drawn back while still maintaining the advantage.
- *Equal opportunities*
  If negotiating with more than one supplier, offer equal opportunities to each to improve their deal. Be fair.
- *Confidentiality*
  Respect a supplier's confidentiality and make a supplier aware that you will not disclose any information received.
- *Correct level of authority*
  Ensure you are negotiating with someone with the authority to make decisions and agree to your requests.
- *Maintaining control*
  Maintain control of negotiations and yourself at all times. Continual questioning will provide you with all the control you need.
- *Being yourself*
  Be yourself, act naturally and enjoy the negotiations. Don't try and add humour if it does not come naturally, but equally don't be over-serious.

Dont's

- *Giving information*
  Don't give a supplier any more information than is required for him to improve his deal. Never disclose the details of one supplier's proposals to another.
- *Assumptions*
  Don't assume anything.
- *Pregnant pauses*
  Don't feel uncomfortable for the supplier. If there is a pregnant pause and it is his turn . . . wait.
- *Buying signals*
  Never give buying signals such as:
  'When we place the contract . . . .'
  'We haven't spoken to anyone else . . . .'
  'Yours is a good deal! . . . .'
  'You are the first person to offer that . . . .'
- *Promises*
  Never make promises that you cannot keep to improve a deal. Don't make statements on future potential business unless you are sure they are correct, and never guarantee future business on the strength of one contract.

Tying up loose ends

The final stages of a negotiation could be the initial stages of the next negotiation. It is important therefore to finalise what you have agreed while paving the way for future discussions.

Confirming the agreement

Confirm in detail, verbally and in writing, what you have agreed and ensure that all parties clearly understand their obligations.

Closing the deal

State that you have reached agreement and that negotiations are complete. Provide everyone with the opportunity to have a final say or make any comments.

The next negotiation

Consider the next negotiation and don't close the door on any opportunities:

When will you meet again?
What will you discuss?
What will you be looking for or monitoring in time for the next meeting?
Does the contract allow you to discuss price?
What changes in the market can affect your agreed deal?

Debriefing

When the final deal has been agreed, take the opportunity to have a debriefing session with the negotiation teams:

What worked well?
What did not work well?
What are future responsibilities?
Are there any concerns?
Is any other work required?

By recording the result of the debriefing session you can set the scene for the next negotiation.

Checklist

- Identify the competition.
- Gather information.
- Set objectives.
- Select the negotiation team and identify roles.
- Arrange meetings.
- Confirm agreement.
- Close the deal.
- Debrief.

6
CONTRACTS

This chapter primarily deals with the benefits a purchasing department could receive from the use of well-constructed contracts, and the results which can be achieved by working with a legal representative. It is not about the construction of contracts or how to negotiate them.

In your quest to become a more proactive, professional buyer you will need to make a number of fundamental decisions, one of which is to become *more* involved with the creation of commercial contracts. There are at least three good reasons for doing this:

(1) As part of your strategy, it will enable you to broaden your overall purchasing knowledge and therefore your cost-effective influence.
(2) Having gained or obtained access to legal expertise, you will be able to extend the range of services you can offer to your clients.
(3) In large companies this will help to relieve pressure on busy legal departments and in smaller organisations it will help to reduce the cost of solicitors' fees, etc.

The starting point for this is the introduction of model forms of contracts.

Model contracts

Model contracts are not a new concept, and are certainly not unique. There are three relevant models to consider:

- purchase of physical products
- purchase of services
- licences for software.

Each individual model represents a list of standard requirements specific to each of the three categories.
For instance, the basic requirements of a product purchase contract could contain:

- definitions
- scope
- duration
- risk/property
- purchase price
- supplier's obligations
- confidentiality of service
- your company's obligations
- termination
- force majeure
- liquidated damages
- waiver
- assignment
- operational procedures
- jurisdiction
- full specification
- appendices to the contract.

Successful model contracts should be written in plain English so that everybody can understand the obligations and implications, they should be fair and reasonable to both parties, and they should lay great emphasis upon the product specification, as no contract, however tight, will protect a loose specification. Therefore everybody needs to take care.

Benefits

Model contracts have a number of significant advantages: the buyer does not reinvent the wheel every time a product is purchased; a model contract ensures consistency of approach, with adherence to agreed quality standards; and it increases the confidence of the legal people in the buyer's ability to protect the company contractually.

Drawbacks

However, there are also a few drawbacks to using model contracts. These mainly surround the chances of buyers acquiring 'tunnel vision' by just filling in the appropriate blank spaces in a model contract, instead of thinking for themselves. Furthermore, as company requirements change and the industrial sector changes, model contracts become out of date.

Both these drawbacks are capable of being addressed without great difficulty. It requires vigilance on the part of each buyer and purchasing management to assess any opportunities which exist in each situation *before* referring to the model contract.

Not every supplier is happy about accepting model contracts, and any variations requested then become a matter of negotiation.

Liaison with the lawyers

At the end of the day, the legal representatives carry the final responsibility for all contractual dealings throughout the company. However, through agreement and a close working relationship, they should be able to delegate much of the responsibility for commercial contractual dealings to the purchasing function. You need to discuss any material variations with the legal people as a matter of standard quality practice. Again, this will give them confidence that you know how far you can negotiate on legal topics before involving them.

This delegated responsibility will allow you to extend your immediate services to the client, and thereby extend your sphere of influence.

As explained earlier, one of your original fundamental decisions was to become more involved with the creation of contracts. This is part of an overall strategy of increasing the involvement and influence of your purchasing function on the expenditure of the company. Since freedom in contractual dealings on behalf of the company is a way to extend purchasing's added value, it is essential to convince the legal representatives to allow you a level of freedom.

Controls

Any effective manager should delegate work to a member of his staff (or to another department) only if he feels that the other party has the necessary training and expertise to carry out the functions successfully, and that there is some mechanism for the manager to retain overall responsibility and a mechanism to receive feedback on the area delegated. Otherwise, he would be irresponsible in his duties and therefore should not delegate.

In securing some level of legal freedom, it is first necessary to convince the lawyers that you, and your staff, have sufficient background training in contract law, over and above the short courses which are available.

The second obstacle to overcome is to create a kind of mutually acceptable control mechanism. This will allow purchasing the freedom to negotiate contracts in their own right, but retain the confidence of the legal function that they would be made aware of any relevant areas. This is where model contracts come into their own, combined with frequent liaison.

The freedom to prepare and negotiate contracts in their own right is essential to increasing the status, influence and cost-effective involvement of purchasing. Otherwise, for one of its main selling points – contract expertise – it will always be perceived by the client as being an adjunct of another department, always having to refer.

Through the use of model contracts you should be able to secure agreement that purchasing may negotiate any contracts based upon the models without any necessary reference to the lawyers beyond the previously agreed regular liaison meetings. This approach will increase the level of communication, contact and confidence. It will also provide a valuable source of information, since the lawyers are potentially privy to corporate plans and areas of expenditure unbeknown to purchasing.

Liaison with the audit department

In a similar way, befriending the company auditor can bring its rewards.

First, having become a centre of influence and gained the trust and respect of clients through your work, it is essential that you maintain these high standards. It is then useful to have the audit department review the 'before and after' situation to show how you have improved the costs profile of your client's department.

Secondly, access by the auditors to the information and standards used by you may help the audit department to add further value to the working operations of the client. This should never be seen as a 'help the snooper' exercise, but should be regarded as work of mutual benefit.

Contract compilation

Although there are many other texts which are specifically devoted to contract construction, it may be useful to say a few words on the subject.

Purpose of the contract

The purpose of a contract is to place business on a fair, reasonable, competitive and cost-effective basis.

Relationship to specification

The most important part of the contract is the specification. This should detail who does what, when, where, and everything else to do with what is being delivered. The construction of the specification is the responsibility of the user, since he is in the prime position of knowing (or should know) what he wants, where he wants it, and how many he wants. The buyer rarely is.

Lack of effort or constructive thought results in bad specifications being produced – for example, vague quality standards – with the users vainly hoping that things can be sorted out at the end, which creates lots of heartache and needless expense. Another fallacy is that the contract will protect a less than comprehensive specification – wrong!

Involvement of the user

As a matter of communication and client confidence, you should be quite open with users in the way you construct contracts. It is a mistake to keep anybody in the dark, especially those who have a major impact on the outcome (successful or otherwise) of a contract project. This shares the information but equally shares the responsibility.

More than one pair of eyes

Contrary to popular rumour in some organisations, buyers are human! Therefore, it is essential to have a procedure whereby at least one other person, preferably another buyer, sees the contract before it is finalised. This is not showing a lack of confidence, but is a way of looking after each other's interests for the combined benefit of all buyers.

Building a contract library

Once you have started preparing and working with contracts, you will need an effective method of holding and accessing your contracts – a contract library.

There are several features of a contract library which will prove extremely useful in your quest to add greater value. These are detailed in the following pages.

ARE YOU MANAGING PURCHASING?

More than one pair of eyes

Centre of influence

Buyers are always fighting for recognition. One of the ways to improve the perception of existing or potential clients is to be seen as the custodian of very important company property – commercial contracts.

It is interesting how people will willingly ask you to hold contracts (which hitherto you might not have known about or been denied access to) if they believe you have a facility to protect and hold them securely. This information can of course lead you into many areas of opportunity for involvement. What you are beginning to accumulate is live data on all the expenditure in the company. Information like this means further opportunities to influence.

Automatic review

Being custodian of these contracts brings with it privileges, responsibilities and opportunities. Built into procedures should be an automatic notification of review at set times prior to the expiry of a contract. For contracts longer than 12 months, there could be an automatic review reminder 12 months after the contract start date.

This automatic review provides both buyer and client with the opportunity to prepare for the expiry of a contract. Expiry dates can slip by without anybody noticing, with work being done out of contract with all the potential problems this can bring.

The automatic review also reminds the client that the purchasing department is still looking after his interests, although the initial project was completed many months before.

The buyer is given an easier way of 'gaining entry' to a client after a number of months' absence, as well as the chance to check out what other expenditure is taking place within any one particular area which he can get usefully involved in.

By knowing the expiry and renewal dates of all contracts, including those in which you were not originally involved, you have an *ideal* opportunity to plan and prepare alternative strategies, which can then be presented to the client. Given the work you have already done, the client is unlikely to want to proceed without your involvement; so you have extended your influence yet further.

Maintain accuracy

If you are going to make the most of the opportunities afforded by the contract library, your clients will expect you to maintain its accuracy. You will be asking them to trust you to advise them of key dates and information. Make a mistake, miss an expiry date, and this could seriously damage your reputation and influence.

It is essential for you to establish procedures very early on for inputting contracts to the library, dealing with updates of information, dealing with changes brought about by reviews/expiry and dealing with information which should be archived or perhaps eventually destroyed.

Stringent though it may seem, you should once again talk to your friendly auditor and invite him informally to review your contract holding procedures and then, once you are sure of gaining a clean bill of health, invite audit to complete a full formal review.

Now, proudly wearing your metaphorical 'I have been audited' badge, you will be able to request copies of contracts with complete confidence, as it is quite likely that their current resting place and attendant administrative procedures have not received the 'laying on of hands' by the auditor.

Conclusion

At the start of this chapter we set out to establish how the purchasing department could become more involved with the creation of a few model contracts with which the lawyers would be happy to delegate some responsibility to the buyers. Not a vast triumph in itself, you might have thought. However, we have seen how this can lead, step by step, to a most powerful position of contract knowledge through the establishment of a contract library.

Checklist

- You need to be involved in the creation of your own commercial contracts.

- As the first step, set up model contracts with legal help.

- Work with your legal department to establish agreement and confidence.

- Ensure controls are in place which provide freedom to your department.

- Make specifications the responsibility of the user (client).

- Set up a contract library to provide:
  – a centre of influence
  – opportunities for review.

7
QUALITY IN PURCHASING

Defining 'quality' can be a full-time occupation, because everyone has their own view of what is a quality product or service.

What is quality?

Understandably therefore, a number of standards have been established which attempt to proceduralise and define quality in a consistent manner. The best known of these are ISO and BS standards. Indeed, some large manufacturers have devised their own standards, which suppliers are required to meet. Many of these standards are specific to certain products or industries, while others deal in general with the procedures and systems surrounding the management of quality – BS5750, for example.

Consider using the motto 'simplest is best', so, for your purposes, the definition to use is,

'Quality is Conformance to Requirements.'

If what your client gets is what he thought he was going to get, that is quality! If what he wants is also what he really needs, then that is true quality; although that is perhaps the subject of another book. Suffice it for now to aim at meeting your clients' wants.

Why is quality important?

Quite simply, the future of your organisation is dependent on bought-in goods and services. All purchased goods and services in some way contribute to the end-product of your organisation. Whether it is a raw material or component which forms an integral part of your product or service, or the standard of meal provided by the contract caterer, they each have an impact on your business and could seriously affect staff morale!

Examples like these illustrate how sub-standard quality can impact on the quality of goods and services you supply to *your* customers – either by affecting the physical quality and performance of your products, or by affecting the attitudes of the people who make the products or provide the service.

The repercussions can, of course, be quite serious. Time is spent detecting poor quality, returning items to suppliers and chasing replacements. Adjustments may need to be made to your systems and equipment to accommodate variations in quality, and even then defects may occur in your products either during or after production. Finally, customers receive poor goods or services from you . . . and then don't come back!

Poor quality which needs remedial work and effort adds significantly to the cost of processing. Aim to add value within your organisation, not cost!

QUALITY IN PURCHASING

Quality of support services

Quality is not only crucial for the item concerned, but must be inherent in the support services that surround the provision of the product or service:

- Is the paperwork accurate? Does the invoice match the delivery note, and does this in turn match the purchase order?
- Does all the supplier's paperwork marry up with yours? Does it need to?
- If there is a query, is the response timely and accurate?

The physical product may be perfect, but if the administration behind it lets you down, the impact can be just as serious.

Every minute you spend chasing somebody, solving problems, rectifying poor quality, is a minute when you are not contributing to your organisation's key objective – generally making money! Your time, and that of everyone else involved in sorting out problems, costs your organisation money in terms of actual costs and lost opportunities.

Quality is two-way

If a purchasing department expects to receive quality services and products from suppliers, it must be prepared to produce and maintain the highest possible standards of quality in its day-to-day dealings with those suppliers. For example:

- Purchase order documentation must be accurate (that means 100 per cent!)
- Correspondence should contain no mistakes and should be addressed correctly – you know how you

- feel if someone spells your name incorrectly or gets your job title wrong!
- The highest possible professional and ethical standards must be maintained when dealing with suppliers.
- All agreements must be honoured, including *payment on time*.

One of the prime laws of quality must be to get your own house in order first! This means continually looking inwards at your own standards and operations before criticising those of your suppliers.

Improving quality

First, it is important to understand the concept of 'total cost of acquisition'. The cost of buying something is not merely the cost stated on the purchase order or invoice, but can include most of the following:

- the buyer's time
- administration resource
- receipt and inspection time
- invoice processing
- cost of payment – cheque, direct debit, etc.

and that is when things go to plan!

If, however, the quality of product or service supplied is not what you require, then add most of the following:

- additional buyer and possibly management time to sort out the problem
- additional administration resource
- progress chasing/expediting
- costs of rejection
- impact of late deliveries, cost of replacements or rescheduling production

- invoice queries due to incorrect paperwork, resulting in additional work

and, most importantly:

- similar costs incurred by your supplier, which *will be passed on to you.*

Secondly, you, as a buyer, must encourage your user departments to specify the quality of goods and services required in the clearest possible terms. How can suppliers be expected to provide the quality you require if you don't tell them?

Establish a level playing field, where both sides know clearly what they are expected to do, and you will find that the increased levels of understanding mean many quality issues simply disappear – or rather they are met and therefore do not become issues.

Measurement

Do you need to measure yourself? If you are not measured, how do you know that you are achieving your objectives and moving forward?

In purchasing, the most obvious measure is the amount of company money being saved as a direct result of your involvement. For instance, you may have helped save £100,000 on the acquisition of new plant or computer equipment.

This is fine, but you can broaden the measurement criteria to show a better picture. Equating savings to company profit as a percentage of annual turnover can be very powerful. For example:

Saving is £100,000
Company annual profit expressed as a percentage of turnover is 10%

ARE YOU MANAGING PURCHASING?

Quality measurement

Therefore additional turnover required to generate additional £100,000 profit is £1 million!

So, you can show that spending £100,000 less with your suppliers is effectively equivalent to doing another £1,000,000 worth of business with your customers. **Never forget**: all expenditure comes out of company profit – it is hard earned; it should be grudgingly spent.

Savings

A saving is simply the difference between an original offer and the final deal which has been effected directly by your involvement.

The problem in using savings as a measure of effectiveness is identifying the original offer or starting point. A straightforward question such as 'Can you reduce your price?' may result in an immediate reduction. However, there will be some doubt that it can be attributed to your skills as a negotiator. Alternatively, it could be argued that the question would not have been asked if you were not involved.

You have to be comfortable with the savings you are recording and be confident that they are directly attributable to your involvement. The question should be, how much would the company have paid if I had not been involved?

Recording

If financial savings are to be used as a measure they must be recorded consistently across the purchasing department.

It is advisable to create a standard format for recording savings to ensure the same criteria are used. The form could document:

- product/service
- original offer
- final deal
- notional savings
- current year and subsequent years' savings
- summary explanation.

Specification changes

Monetary savings can be achieved by changing a specification. The specification is the responsibility of your client and you cannot therefore affect it during negotiation.

If a specification change instigated by your client results in a reduction in price then all well and good, but this cannot be considered a saving as a result of purchasing involvement unless the initiative came from you – in which case you might feel that the client would not have reviewed the specification had you not encouraged such a review.

Savings v. budgets

If a supplier's initial offer is £x under budget, this cannot be claimed as a purchasing saving. It is a saving as far as the company is concerned in so far as it will not have to spend as much as planned, but that part of the overall saving is not due to the involvement of purchasing. For example:

Office chairs: Budget   £150 each
                Initial offer £140
                Final deal   £128

Although the company will save £22 on each chair purchased that year, purchasing can really only take credit for the last £12 on the final deal. On the other hand, it might be that you sourced the market and found a new supplier as an alternative to the organisation which had been supplying your company for many years.

It is difficult to establish hard-and-fast rules. The point to remember is that there is nothing to be gained by trying to claim financial savings greater than your clients feel is reasonable.

Remember, when it comes to quality, perception is everything. And, quality of savings is no exception.

Feedback

You will need to find out how well you and your team are doing, there's no better way than asking the client for feedback on quality performance.

Set up separate sessions outside of project work and discuss in detail how well a piece of work was handled. Consider points such as:

- understanding of objectives
- communications
- timeliness
- attitude during the project
- overall end-result.

Openly invite feedback and encourage your client to give an honest opinion.

The response you receive should help you assess current standards and pinpoint specific areas in which improvements can be made. This effort will go some way to enhancing purchasing's reputation and standing within your company.

Only by inviting feedback from your client can you be sure you are fulfilling your role.

When to obtain feedback

By inviting verbal feedback *during* projects you give your client the opportunity to express views and concerns. These can then be discussed and action taken if necessary.

It is also advisable to invite general feedback *at the end* of each project, so that you can be sure that your client is satisfied with your involvement. By doing this you can develop an action plan to ensure future involvement with that client.

Reacting to feedback

Once feedback on your performance is received, react to it quickly where necessary. If negative comments are made, discuss them with your client to agree how improvements can be made.

If you do not react to feedback there is no point in asking for it, and it will not be long before your credibility suffers as a result and clients go back to buying their own goods and services.

Also bear in mind that, every time you meet a client to discuss past work, you have an opportunity to learn of future plans and therefore another possible opportunity for involvement.

Checklist

- Quality is receiving what you need.

- Be aware that poor quality adds to costs – directly and indirectly.

- Support services and administration form part of the delivery of goods and/or services so must be of a high quality – from both you and your suppliers.

- Get your own house in order first.

- Understand the total cost of acquisition.

- Specify the quality required so both parties understand what is expected.

- Work *with* your suppliers to improve quality.

8
ENVIRONMENTAL ISSUES

Today, most organisations are coming under increasing pressure to ensure that their practices and products are 'environmentally friendly'. Purchasing departments are therefore being asked that the products and services they buy conform to this friendliness. But how do you find out what is 'environmentally friendly' and, perhaps more importantly, what is unfriendly?

Sources of information

There are now a number of well-established pressure groups, most of which are willing to provide guidelines on issues such as recycling, waste management, effective use of materials, and so on. Perhaps the most well known of these is Friends of the Earth (26–28 Underwood Street, London N1 7JQ) which provides a wide range of practical guidelines.

In addition, many trade and professional bodies now offer advice and expertise, although understandably the subject matter is restricted to their own industries.

The 'green' issue is a highly emotive one and it is essential that the purchasing department retains an objective viewpoint – hence the need to gather as much information as possible. Find out the *facts*. If, however,

Making a contribution

you are unable to find third party advice or information, the golden rule is 'use your common sense'.

Why is environment important?

Like it or not, as a buyer you are also a consumer. Some consumers, of course, are bigger than others, but, no matter how small a consumer you are, you have obligations to ensure that your actions and decisions are 'responsible' when they impact on the environment.

The obligations may stem from peer pressure, a desire for positive public relations or simply a personal preference to contribute to the advances being made on environmental issues. More likely, as a buyer representing an organisation, you (and the organisation) will be influenced and governed by the increasingly complex legislative structure being built within the UK and EC.

As pressures increase from both inside and outside your organisation, previously ignored environmental issues are pushing themselves to the front.

Your contribution

As a buyer, you will need to assume many roles when dealing with these environmental issues. Three key ones are: arbiter, communicator and promoter.

Arbiter

No-one is closer to the marketplace than the buyer. You must be prepared to assume the role of 'honest broker' when it comes to deciding whether something is environmentally friendly or not, and whether a product or service falls within the framework of any relevant UK and EC legislation.

A great many supply companies are jumping on the bandwagon, claiming their products are 'green'. Most are, and are making genuine attempts to improve their environmental acts, but many are simply using the current surge of interest in the environment as a marketing tool. Buyers must be in a position to assess objectively the *genuinely* green products and services.

Communicator

Most environmentally friendly products and services are currently selling at a premium. This is either due to the fact that suppliers are pricing at what the market will bear, or more likely due to the fact that the technology and processes involved in 'decreasing unfriendliness' are currently more expensive than traditional processes.

Faced with a potential choice of, say,

Product A – not 'green' and less expensive or
Product B – 'green' and more expensive,

the purchasing department must communicate all the facts and information to the user departments that set the specification, and to the organisation as a whole.

The difference between 'green' and 'not green' may be genuine but, on the other hand, it may just be perceptual. Such a difference must be quantified and costed. The decision must then fall to the user who defined the specification or to the organisation as a whole to decide policy; for example, if a premium is to be paid (where it exists).

Promoter

Buyers have a responsibility to promote the use of good environmental practices by their suppliers – effective use of packaging, professional waste management, correct use of durables and cleaning materials, and so on.

Once again, there is an opportunity for the proactive, professional buyer to be seen as the centre of competence in this area. You can promote environmental awareness amongst your clients and then be the person best placed to help them to act/buy in a responsible manner.

Checklist

- Be aware that environmental issues will affect you, and that pressure will come from inside and outside your organisation.

- Gather the facts.

- Arbitrate objectively, not emotionally.

- Communicate the facts.

- Encourage good environmental practices by your suppliers.

9
TRAINING AND DEVELOPMENT

Training of purchasing staff is often centred around the skills they need in negotiation and contract law. While this approach is valuable it tends to be quite narrow in outlook. It consequently misses out the valuable opportunities provided through training in areas such as consultancy, team building, interpersonal and presentational skills. These skills will assist development in the area of people contact, which is a high proportion of the purchasing activity used by successful buyers.

Where to start

Start by recognising that any training programme is an investment, since the objective is to help people improve their performance and to realise their full potential. Then link those objectives to company requirements so that they have a specific purpose. Having identified individual and team training needs, plan the training programme, allowing time for pre- and post-course training. Lastly, evaluate the training over the next few months. What were the results? Is there a difference in performance? What was the overall value?

Training should ultimately provide a benefit both to the individual and to the purchasing area and to this end you will need to discuss the expectations of any training you undertake and agree how you will follow it through at the end of the whole training programme. The key learning objectives should be achievable, time bound and measurable.

Training needs

Identification of training needs takes time. You have to be working with people for a reasonable period before you can begin to evaluate their development potential. Consider following a development programme which identifies the key requirements of the job – the areas that fall short of the standard will indicate where the training emphasis should be placed.

Regular annual appraisal of performance is another valuable tool in assessing development, and if this is coupled with regular development discussions (say bi-monthly) then the progress of purchasing staff (as for any staff) can be monitored and evaluated to everyone's benefit.

Planning

Training shouldn't be rushed, and whether it's in-house or external the programme needs commitment both in time and people. The capacity of the individual undertaking the training is also a consideration. There is little point in cramming information into people by organising too tight a programme. People need time to digest what has been learnt rather than dashing off to another course, and time to put the new-found knowledge into practice.

When putting together a training plan, consider all the

opportunities available. Most people look no further than external courses, but the alternatives are numerous. They cover:

- on-the-job training by experienced staff
- audio and video cassettes
- discussion groups (especially feedback sessions with previous clients)
- books (much has been written about the theory of purchasing)
- visits to other companies (much can be learnt from just talking to other buyers).

The self-help options are particularly useful as they allow people to learn at their own pace and to revisit any of the areas of which they are unsure. In larger companies, the personnel department may well run various personal development courses which would be of great benefit. Finally, the Institute of Purchasing and Supply can provide much information.

Because training is an investment for the future, once the plan is in place only acts of God should cause a cancellation! So often work takes precedence over a training programme, generally because of a reactive attitude.

Training relies on commitment and time from other people. Cancellations do not project a very professional image of you or your team – they also cost money.

Reinvesting the techniques

Having completed a particular training programme it is all too easy not to use the techniques and ideas you have learnt. There is an old quip among the farmers of Virginia:

> A group of young turkeys went on a training course to learn how to fly and spent three days

successfully performing the techniques. At the end of the course they all walked home!

To make sure this doesn't happen to your 'turkeys':

- agree two or three action points following the training programme
- add the action points into your and their personal development programme file or appraisal notes
- present a synopsis of the course to your communication group or management team, tell them what your action points are and let them know what help they can give to assist you in achieving them
- circulate course notes or training ideas to your team/colleagues
- conduct your own debriefing, using the course notes as a group training aid.

Once again, in smaller companies where you might be the only full-time buyer, you will need a lot of self-discipline to ensure that you really do use what you have learnt. It might help to enlist the services of a friend. You should write out a list of key points learnt from your training and then a list of actions or goals to be achieved over the next three to six months. Agree to meet with this friend in three months' and six months' time to discuss how you are progressing. Knowing that you have to meet and explain yourself regularly will act as an extra stimulus to put into practice what you have recently learnt.

Whatever you do, don't waste the opportunities.

Team building

All teams are made up of individuals, so the key to the success of a larger group is to complement individual skills to create an effective team. The key elements in building an effective team are:

Team building

- open and honest communication among all team members, with mistakes being treated as learning opportunities
- healthy competition within the team, with suggestions and ideas being developed quite freely
- a visible pride in the success of the team
- clarity about objectives and how they are to be achieved
- an openness to invite others into the group to discuss ideas and solicit help
- regular reviews of performance, objectives, standards and procedures
- training and development are seen as an important focus for moving the team forward
- sound relationships with the manager and genuine trust and support on a two-way basis
- a sense of enjoyment within the group, coming from the team spirit being generated and the success being achieved.

Checklist

- Provide a broad base of training.
- Link training to company and team objectives.
- Plan thoroughly for training.
- Reinvest training in all team members.

10
CONSULTANCY WITHIN THE PURCHASING FUNCTION

A purchasing department does not exist by divine right. There is usually no powerful mandate which compels other parts of the organisation to involve purchasing when products or services are required from external suppliers. The only reason why purchasing exists (and should exist) is that it has an expertise in commercial and contractual areas which other departments do not have, and has the potential to add value by their involvement. Even this is not enough. The purchasing department has continually to sell its services and added-value abilities, treating internal users as clients. It has, in fact, to take on the role of an internal consultant.

Many purchasing functions are in this position (whether they know it or not) and need to acquire consultancy skills to increase their effectiveness in their company.

Gaining entry

Earlier in this book we considered the cry, often heard within purchasing departments, 'Why is it nobody knocks on our door asking to use us when they know we can help them?' For many reasons this is an unfortunate fact of life.

If purchasing believes that it can add value by being involved, then it has to find new ways of 'gaining entry' into previously untapped or denied opportunities. Many of the techniques briefly described below are the stock in trade of management consultants and therein lies another source of useful and much-published work.

Expenditure analysis

It is essential for any purchasing consultant to do a lot of groundwork, to find out who spends what with whom. It is surprising the amount of money spent by departments which has previously gone unnoticed. These expenditure analyses can be obtained from your Accounts department, remember it is the point of influence you are after.

Obtaining the first meeting

Trying to obtain a meeting with the head of a department with whom you have never had dealings before, or who doesn't see the need to involve purchasing's expertise in his area of expenditure, may not be easy.

Alternatives to 'cold calling' may be:

- Casual contact – ensuring you are at a meeting or in a place where you can talk to him easily. It only needs a 5 minute conversation to bring about a success – the first meeting.
- Networking – asking one of your satisfied clients to put in a good word for you or allowing you to use his name. This may well pave the way to obtaining that vital first meeting.

Preparation

It is a fact of life that consultants, like purchasing people, are always having to convince clients to use their services. Preparation is therefore crucial. Make sure you 'know your client'; be sure of your facts; consider your method of approach, role and style.

Pitfalls

The old adage 'first impressions count' holds well here. You may only get one chance, and there are some pitfalls to avoid:

- concentrating too hard on selling and not listening enough
- spending too little time finding out about the client
- assuming that the client knows why you are there without testing it, building up false assumptions
- pushing solutions without finding out
- suggesting quick fixes to create impact which doesn't create a long-term solution.

Having established a rapport with your client, it is necessary to agree the ground-rules of your future working relationship – commitments, responsibilities and roles for involvement in any project or level of expenditure. In consultancy parlance this is called 'contracting', which is as good a word as any for purchasing's use.

Contracting

Contracting is the level of expectations you and your client have of each other. Not taking the time to establish a good, well-understood contract with suppliers generally leads to a less than successful conclusion. It is just the same with internal clients.

It is imperative that the consultant and client agree, right from the start, each other's responsibility, scope and method of operating during the project, plus the level of confidentiality required. It may appear that establishing these issues is a matter of common sense, but think how often purchasing staff have misinterpreted user requirements.

It is essential to keep re-establishing the 'contract' between client and consultant, to ensure that everybody understands the ground-rules. Again, do not make promises or agree to amendments which are impossible to fulfil.

Choosing a style

In consultancy terms, there are three major styles which can be usefully adopted by purchasing staff:

- expert
- pair of hands
- collaborative.

The key is knowing which style is appropriate at any one time and agreeing this with your client.

Expert role

This is where the consultant takes control of the process, perhaps by leading the negotiation or preparing the contract. The client places himself directly in the hands of the consultant, and the consultant takes total responsibility.

Pair of hands

This is a 'do it as I tell you role': the client takes complete control, and there is no discretion. The importance of this is that the client takes full responsibility for the actions and outcomes.

It is essential for the buyer to avoid becoming a scapegoat for things going wrong which were outside his brief and therefore his discretion. Unclear information in proposal responses to a badly worded specification, set up by the client but sent out by the buyer, is such an example.

Be very careful before accepting a brief to be simply an extra pair of hands for the client. It doesn't sit easily alongside your claim to be a professional purchasing consultant.

Collaborative

This is the more common of the roles. The client and the buyer share the responsibility, commitment and tasks involved.

Depending on the original contract, buyers and clients can switch roles through the life of any project, and should do at times. The essence is to agree which role either party

Data gathering: an essential stage

should be playing, otherwise there is no contract and the working relationship breaks down.

Data gathering and problem identification

This is an essential stage of any consultant's work, but in terms of maintaining influence with the user certain elements have to be considered.

Facts v. assumptions!

It is essential for the buyer to test out all the preconceived notions of the user. Relying on assumptions leads only to heartache and disappointment.

What data are needed?

The buyer will be greatly relied upon in assessing what data (e.g. competitive quotes) may be needed to give the client a full cost picture. The buyer's ability and commercial acumen will be called upon.

How are the data to be presented?

If it is the buyer's responsibility to present (let's say) a conclusion from a competitive quote exercise, he must decide what method is going to be most readily received by his client. This may not be the easiest way for the buyer to present data. A great many excellent buying projects have failed through lack of effective and relevant presentation to the client.

Apart from costs, which will be important to all clients, controls/security/technical aspects will be of most interest to the computer department, appearance/motivational aspects to marketing clients, and so on.

Problem-solving

The purchasing solution to problems may not be the one that is best received or even recognised by the client. An example is the open quotation and negotiation process, which may be one with which the client is completely unfamiliar and consequently uncomfortable with and therefore rejects. However, from an overall company viewpoint, this may be the most cost-effective method of producing a solution. The purchasing consultant has to sell his solution and carry out a keen balancing act.

Disengagement

This is a wonderful term, and means that, having finished a project or reached the end of a particular assignment, the purchasing consultant must not 'hang about'; he has responsibilities elsewhere. This relates primarily to project work, but also extends to long-term production purchasing as well.

Once the purchasing exercise is over, agree with the client a clean cut-off date – the contract completion. Even on production line purchasing, most jobs have an end-date, even if it is not immediately apparent.

Make sure that all your work has been fully documented and a copy left with the client. Even if the work seemed to be 'one-off' it's amazing how similar situations subsequently arise and your notes would be useful.

Feedback

Feedback, it is said, is the food of champions. To increase the value of the purchasing department, it is essential that it receives honest and factual feedback on projects purchasing exercises it has carried out. This data will provide something to build on, to amplify successes and to rectify mistakes.

Referrals

At the end of a purchasing exercise, always question whether there are further opportunities for involvement. This may be in the same or a related area or any other known area of the company. Referrals are easier than 'cold calling' your potential clients.

Summing up, as budgets are getting tighter and all company cost centres are being scrutinised, the purchasing department will need to make a stand on added value. Like most consultancies, the potential benefit in involvement will have to be sold aggressively.

The ultimate client

With experience, and having mastered many of the management consultant's skills and techniques, you will be able not only to produce a good local purchasing solution for your immediate client, but also to ensure that you have maximised the saving/benefit for your ultimate client – the company.

At first sight these would seem to be one and the same thing. Indeed, they rarely consciously oppose each other. However, in addition to achieving a local saving by purchasing the client's specification in the best possible manner (and therefore better than he would be able to do himself), you will be able to discuss his initial specification, understanding how his requirements relate to his work and staff, and then be able to offer alternatives – or, better still, merely ask questions about how certain aspects of the specification produce benefits for the company. You will be able to lead your departmental client to the realisation that certain initial requirements were not in fact essential and that an amended specification could be possible. The real trick is not to purchase a fleet of vans on the best possible terms if in fact you could negotiate a 24-hour courier contract at better terms. This is the often unseen additional corporate saving which can be obtained by experienced purchasing consultants. However, it takes time and a lot of close working with clients to build that level of trust and openness so that you can freely discuss sensible alternatives without your client feeling in anyway threatened.

Checklist

- Consider the skills of consultancy to develop internal purchasing involvement.

- Do your homework on the client to prepare for the meeting.

- Choose a consultancy style which is appropriate.

- Agree early in the process the roles you will perform in supporting the client.

- Ask for feedback as a means of continuous improvement.

- Remember, the ultimate client is the company you work for – add profit, not cost.

11
TIPS FOR SMALL SUPPLIERS

It is with some trepidation that we attempt to pass on information which will help suppliers have more success in making headway with large organisations – including our own. However, there is nothing worse than being on the receiving end of a continual stream of calls from new salesmen who have just discovered the existence of Yellow Pages or to watch ill-prepared reps die on their feet when faced with an experienced professional buying team. So, spurred by a mixture of deep moral feelings of fairness and a selfish wish to have less of our time wasted in the future, we humbly offer the following to all suppliers.

A large part of the UK supplier base is made up of what can be called 'small companies' employing fewer than twenty people. These organisations provide *vital* supply services. However, much benefit is lost and cost added by large buyers and small suppliers failing to communicate with each other effectively. There are a number of ways to ease these difficulties, which are portrayed as buyers helping suppliers to help each other.

Small Business Enterprises

Short-distance supply lines for buyers can be effective. A problem for buyers is knowing what suppliers/customers are available on the doorstep. Small Business Enterprises (SBEs), in whatever form they appear, hold large amounts of information on potential customers for any product or service within the locality. Likewise the SBEs hold a database of all available suppliers registered with them for particular product lines.

In addition to holding such registers, SBEs actively promote increased communication by arranging buyers' exhibitions. These are events whereby SBEs make forums/facilities available to 'buying companies' to present themselves to the potential small supplier. This maximises the potential for the right supplier to get in touch with the right buyer.

Another advantage of the SBEs is that they generally have access to large companies, and are aware of the most effective route for any enquiry. Unfortunately, in our experience many small companies do not become aware of this process until too late, when the search for potential business may get lost in the all too inevitably complex structure of large companies.

Generally, the onus of making buyers aware of the benefit of new products and services falls on the supplier, so the importance of the 'approach' is dealt with next.

Approaching large companies

The rule of thumb which should be adopted is to contact the person who would be most interested in your product or service. Writing to the Chief Executive or the Purchasing Manager, when you really want the Senior Buyer responsible for stationery, wastes everybody's time and money. Take the time to find out. Again, your local SBE may be able to help.

How to make contact

Having found the correct person to contact, is it better to write, telephone or turn up on the doorstep on the off chance of seeing the buyer?

It is probably always better to telephone. There are a number of reasons:

- everybody is busy, and letters take time to read
- phone calls are immediate
- letters can be impersonal, phone calls are less so
- there is a better chance of setting up a meeting there and then, which should be the main aim of the supplier.

Although there are disadvantages to phoning – the person not being there or not ringing back – the advantages outweigh the disadvantages in the long term.

Never call on the off chance. It is the worst way to represent anybody's company, and wastes people's time, which means money. Even if the buyer has the time to see such a caller, the 'off the cuff' approach is not likely to be met with great attention and shows to the buyer a lack of professionalism. The comment 'as I was in the area' holds little credibility. However, calling in to a reception to find out the name of the correct person to contact is an excellent way of preparing the ground.

Setting up meetings

The methods of effectively setting up meetings on the phone are too numerous to mention. There are courses run by SBEs which deal with this subject in depth. Suffice to say that, like suppliers, buyers have conflicting demands on their time, and meeting suppliers is just one of them.

It is necessary for the small supplier to make it as easy

and as cost-effective as possible for the buyer to meet him. Short meetings, well prepared in advance, are nearly always well received.

Dealing with rejection

No matter how professional the approach, or how beneficial the product/service, you will inevitably meet with rejection at some time. It is a numbers game: there is a ratio of calls to appointments to sales. Depending upon the industry concerned, your company's standing within that industry and your personal effectiveness, these 'odds' will shorten or lengthen, meaning fewer or greater numbers of calls per eventual sale.

Always remember that rejection is time bound. What is wrong today can be right tomorrow. If rejected, always find out as much as possible about:

- the buyer's use of their current product/service
- when the existing contract expires
- when is the best time to make another approach
- who else might be interested.

Rejection isn't a happy feeling, but the supplier should always leave the buyer with:

- a sense of the supplier's professionalism and credibility
- a willingness at least to meet again some time in the future.

Rejection is tough, but it is also a learning process.

Professionalism

Generally, small suppliers have the advantage of, amongst other things, flexibility, availability and lack of bureaucracy. But they also sometimes lack the financial standing, quality of presentation and confidence which larger companies have, as well as having fewer in-house resources to call upon.

When placing orders, the smaller supplier's confidence plays a significant part in the decision by the buyer. What can the smaller company do about this?

Preparation

Before entering any meeting it is important to know as much as possible about the company's buying policies and to anticipate all questions on technical matters, applications of the product/service, back-up personnel and all matters relating to the company, its staff, etc.

Quality

Everything about the supplier's company should demonstrate quality, from the initial presentation to the final documentation. It is likely that any supplier will get one chance. First impressions count, so make the most of it. You only get one chance to make a good first impression!

Presentation

Practice until the presentation becomes word-perfect and all the presentation brochures, etc. are displayed in the correct manner. There is nothing worse than to sit through a fumbled presentation; it rocks everybody's confidence.

Promises

The world is strewn with one-hit wonders, both buyers and suppliers. In their haste to make a sale, suppliers sometimes make promises which they either have no intention of keeping, or plainly cannot keep. Reputations will inevitably be seriously damaged by problems of this kind, especially relating to delivery. Hope is never a good basis for developing or continuing a successful business relationship.

Remember, the buyer has his own clients, so the number of people let down can be enormous. Unless you are sure; don't promise.

Final supply

At the end of the day, fulfilment is what matters. The right product/service, in the right place, at the right time, in the right quantity is the ultimate test – the cost, of course, having been determined earlier.

If there is likely to be any variation, warn the buyer as early as possible. No matter what people say, nobody likes surprises, especially about bad news. Early warning allows alternative action, and retains credibility for the supplier in the eyes of the buyer.

Documentation

Much is said these days about bad debt and late payment, with the emphasis on their effect on the small supplier – and rightly so. However, a reasonable proportion of late payment problems is attributable to suppliers not bothering to find out about and/or not complying with the buying company's payment process. For example, the cheque production computer program may be run only once a month – so it's no good demanding payment within seven days of delivery.

Because getting paid is important, it is essential to find out how to make it easy for the buyer to pay your invoices. The documentation trail – delivery note, purchase order reference, invoice properly completed – is vital to the numerous processes of a large company, especially when this process is computerised.

Buying from local/smaller sources of supply can be cost-effective for large organisations, but small suppliers disregard their large customers' normal ways of doing business at their peril. The opportunity of successful sales is put at risk unless the supplier is fully aware of all the relevant information before concluding any business agreement.

A final word of encouragement

Small, good-quality local suppliers who always deliver on time are not too numerous these days, but, once 'found' by the larger buyers, there is the prospect of long-term business – provided you deliver the goods!

Index

acknowledgements 41
agreements
  confirming 78, 80
  honouring 41
  meeting terms 51
  working 41
arbiter of environmental
  issues, role as 107, 108
assertiveness 19
assumptions 64, 74–5, 77
audit
  department, liaison
    with 85–6
  fees 27
  trail 41, 42–3
automation 23
authority
  limits, internal 43
  in negotiation 76

bank charges 27, 56
bargaining 71
BS standards 93
budgets 100–1
buying signals 77

call-off orders on standing
  contracts 41
casual contact 120
clarification 75
client
  feedback 19, 37, 60, 127,
    129

needs 58, 64
satisfaction 27–8
ultimate 128
coercion 71
cold calling 120, 127
collaboration 123–5
common sense 28, 56
communication 19
  of environmental
    issues 107–10
  skills 28
  team 116
communicator of
  environmental issues,
  role as 107, 108–9
company evaluation 28
competition 29, 39, 66–7,
  80
  supplier 43
  within team 116
compromise 71
computer software
  licences 27
conduct, code of 39, 40
confidentiality 44, 47, 64,
  76
consultancy 119–29
  choosing a style 122–5,
    129
  costs 27
  gaining entry 119–21
  obtaining the first
    meeting 120
  pitfalls 121

(*Consultancy* Cont.)
  preparation 121
  skills 28
contact
  approaching large
    companies 132–4
  casual 120
  how to make 133
contracts 81–92, 122
  automatic review 89–90, 92
  centre of influence 89, 92
  checking 87, 88
  compilation 28, 86–7
  expertise 85
  expiry and renewal
    dates 90
  involvement of the
    user 87
  maintaining accuracy 90
  model 82–3
  purpose of 86
  relationship to
    specification 86
  reviews 28, 90
  written 41
contract law 85
contract library 87–90, 91, 92
controls 37, 41–3, 47
  client 123
  contract 84–5
  negotiation 76
costs
  consultancy 27
  of poor quality 103
  of poor service 20
credibility with supplier 50

data
  facts v. assumptions 125
  gathering 124, 125–6

  presentation 126
  requisition 18–19
  type needed 125
debriefing 78–9
delegation 84
deliveries
  expediting 20
  paperwork 19, 41, 95
  timing 19
development 111–17
disengagement 126–7
documentation *see*
  paperwork

effectiveness 37
emotion 71
entertainment 42, 45
environmental issues 105–9
  importance of 107
  sources of
    information 105–7
ethics 39, 43–6, 47
expediting 20, 51–3, 64
expenditure
  analysis 120
  total company 27, 29
  see also costs
expertise of consultant 123

failure, suppliers 62–3
feedback
  client 19, 37, 60, 127, 129
  on colleagues'
    performance 36
  negative 55
  on quality
    performance 101–2
  reacting to 102
  when to obtain 102
final supply 136
financial year, supplier 68

INDEX

gifts 45, 47
goals 17
good practice
 requirements 42

incentives 45, 47
information
 on environmental
  issues 105–7
 gathering for
  negotiation 68, 80
 giving, to supplier 77
 unclear 123
Institute of Purchasing and Supply 113
interest rates 28
Inventory Control system 18
invoicing 41
 matching with delivery note 95
 payment of 19
involvement, early 29–30
ISO standards 93

lawyers, liaison with 84–5
listening 19
 during negotiation 72
logical reasoning 71

management
 of project
  purchasing 34–7
 senior 32
market forces 28
marketing 31
measurement 97–9
medical insurance 27
meetings
 preparation 135
 setting up 133–4
model contracts 82–3

negotiation 19, 28, 29, 65–80, 126
 areas for 73–4
 closing 78, 80
 creating the
  atmosphere 72
 do's and dont's in 76–7
 information gathering for 68
 methods and
  techniques 66
 objectives 65–6, 68–9, 76, 80
 opportunities in 72, 76
 planning the next 78
 preparing for 66–71, 76, 80
 principles of 71–4
 team 69–71, 80
 tying up loose ends 77–9
 win/lose 65–6
 win/win 65–6
networking 120

objectives 17, 26
 negotiation 65–6, 68–9, 76, 80
open quotation 126
order confirmations 41
order processing 20

paperwork 41, 42, 137
 accuracy of 95
 delivery 19
personal conduct 46, 47
personal interests 45–6, 47
persuasion 19, 71
pregnant pauses 77
pre-planning 31
presentation 136
proactive
 purchasing 25–38, 50

141

problem
  identification 125–6
problem-solving 126
product purchasing 17
professionalism 39, 64, 135–7
  standards 43–6
profit 20–1
  margins, supplier 68
project purchasing 20
  management of 34–7
  marketing of 31
  principles of 39–47
project teams 26, 32–3
project variety 34–5
promises 77, 136
promoter of environmental issues, role as 107, 109
purchase orders 18, 41
purchasing brochure 32
purchasing function 26
purchasing
  opportunities 15–17

quality 93–103, 135
  definition 93–4
  importance of 94–6
  improving 96–7
  two-way 95–6
questions
  during negotiation 75
  open 19

recession 15
recording 99–100
recycling 105
referrals 127
rejection, dealing with 134
requisition data 18–19, 41
resource allocation 30
resource scheduling 30
rotation 36

savings 37, 97, 98–101
seminar, supplier 62
sensitivity 28
shortlisting of
  suppliers 58–9
skills 19
Small Business Enterprises 131–2
solicitors' fees 27
specialisation,
  departmental 34
specification changes 100
staff
  recruitment 35
  supplier 57
  see also team
success
  judging 21–2
  suppliers' 62–3
summarising 75
suppliers 41
  competition 43
  financial viability 29
  guarantee 57
  initial contact 54–5
  motivation 61–2, 64
  needs 74
  number of 55–6
  performance 59–63, 64
  measurement 59–60
  measurement criteria 60
  reviews of 61
  selection 28, 52, 53–6
  seminar 62
  shortlisting 58–9
  small 131–7
  staff 57
  success 62–3
  turnover 57, 68
  vetting 56–9, 64
  working with 49–53

INDEX

support services, quality of 95

targets, meeting 19
team
  building 38, 114–16
  negotiating 69–71
  project 32–3
  spirit 35–6, 116
telephone manner 19
terms and conditions 29
  meeting suppliers' 51
timing 19, 98
total cost of acquisition 96
traditional views of purchasing 16, 17–20

training 111–17
  needs 112
  objectives 18, 23
  planning 112–13, 117
  reinvesting techniques 113–14, 117
  starting 111–12
  team building 114–16
turnover, supplier 57, 68
twinning 36

understanding 75

waste management 105
working agreements 41